THE SPICE OF LIFE

HERBS AND SPICES FOR HERITAGE, HEALTH, HEALING AND HOME

SHALAMANTU WISDOM

THE SPICE OF LIFE

Herbs and Spices for Heritage, Health, Healing and Home

Shalamantu Wisdom

CONTENTS

I would like to dedicate this book to All of Creation. What a mystical and wondrous dream which we have been given a chance to explore. Next to that Source Universal Creator Energy, I would like to dedicate this book to my loving parents Joseph and Irene and to my wonderful son Vay. Your support has allowed for new heights of achievement and growth that would not have been the same without your company, guidance and learning/teaching. Thank you for being you and thank you for being here.

The Superfoods Checklist

Foods that Superhumans are made of

This checklist includes:
- Foods that help with brain function
- Cures for viral infections
- Vegetables that help manage stress
- Spices that improve skin health
- And much, much, much more!

This list should be the first part of
everyone's grocery list to transform your
health and your life.

To receive this life changing tool, scan the QR Code or visit the link
www.shalamantu.com/lifeupgrade

"With fresh knowledge, we are able to make different decisions based on that new awareness. When we choose to take action using that new learning, we will create a different outcome. This, my friend, is how we change our destiny. Continue to add greatness to the Mind and it will bring forth many fruitful results. Once we allow ourselves to receive quality information, everything is possible."

— SHALAMANTU

Have you ever looked down at a beautifully prepared meal in front of you and couldn't wait to take a bite of what seems so pleasing to your eyes? Your mind is confident that the first taste of this dish will change your day entirely. Maybe the food has been ordered at a restaurant, or perhaps someone close to you has prepared it in hopes of satisfying your tastebuds. The anticipation is too great, and you can't deny it any longer. You piece off a bite-sized section and aim it towards your mouth. Even the chemicals and hormones in your body are preparing to adjust to this flavor explosion. The utensil hits your lips with a burst of joy. There it is, the first bite!

Here we go! A few chews in, no rapture yet. Maybe it will take a bit longer for the aftertaste to kick in—a couple more chomps. I mean, there is taste there; it's just, well, not what you were expecting. Oh man, how disappointing! High expectations dashed in a matter of moments. It's food, nourishment, and a blessing and all that, but the flavor isn't there. How could this happen? When it comes to the taste of food getting a passing grade, the main factor often has to do with the seasoning.

Here's another scenario. An aroma-filled dish is staring at

you from the table. It looks tremendous. Your pupils and your nostrils convince you of impending satisfaction. You take that first bite, and there it is. Bliss! The food is so good you don't even know what to do with yourself. You melt into the seat; the people around you become less important as the flavor has taken over most of your sensual reality. This meal is too gratifying! It was a game-changer. You may slither over to the nearest comfy area and just let that dish digest for an hour or three.

The food was utterly satisfying to your tongue. But what about the ingredients? Were they packed with flavor but a punishment to your health? Right about now, you might be saying, "who cares, the meal was soooo good. I don't want to think about that right now or ever!" The thing is, though, if you aren't thinking about your health now, the effects WILL creep up on you, and there WILL be a price to pay at some point.

But what if you could have the best of both worlds: Food that tastes so good that it could make a hyena blush, while giving you and your family health and vitality all at the same time. Luckily for humanity, there are foods like this! They have been with us forever. And for many, have been known about and used freely. Today we will find many of them.

We'll be discovering these foods and learning about the positive effects that they will have for us, and there are many. **Flavor and health do NOT have to oppose each other.** They can complement each other, as it should be.

We can explore the history and heritage of these flavorful living legends. We will check out some of the roots of ancient trading and their role within foundational societies. We'll also find out more about how certain foods can give us health and even help heal us. Finally, we can learn to grow and utilize these foods today. We will learn how to store and keep these foods fresh and maximize the flavors stashed within.

My name is Shalamantu. Thank you for taking your health and your tastebuds seriously, or lightly, depending on how you look at it. It is my sincere hope to guide you to a happier, more fulfilling life.

To have a heightened health level, you must know and understand the importance of eating the proper herbs and spices. It can be as simple as identifying which of these foods will work best to help you reach your goals. If this seems like an unimportant thing, it's not! Remember, you are eating each day. And each meal can be healthy and flavorful or bland and unhealthy. The choice is yours. But whatever you choose, it will be A LOT of meals, which adds up.

As a health practitioner for over 30 years, I intend to create the healthiest, most functional body for myself and others. After the tens of thousands of hours of research and just as much or more time exercising, I have made it my life mission to help many others learn the tips and techniques to build the life of their dreams, beginning with physical health. In this book, you will receive the results of my blood, sweat, and tears, which took me decades to learn and achieve. I hope to serve you and help you on the path to higher health regardless of where you're at now. As a personal trainer, dietary 'mad scientist' and life coach, my passion will become a service to your journey to make you and your family healthier, one piece of Wisdom at a time.

This book is a quick, easy, and informative transition into understanding herbs and spices' role in our lives. And an introduction to how we can easily add them into our days. The layout is not like a textbook or a scientific journal. It is simple and fun while helping us understand how this topic can easily change our lives for the better. We use or ingest spices every day in nearly every meal. But we know very little about them and their importance. Here we re-introduce ourselves to our old friends, the spice and the herb, starting with our rich heritage and why they became so important in our lives. Enjoy the ride!

"Once you get a spice in your home, you have it

forever. Women never throw out spices.
Egyptians were buried with their spices. I
know which one I am taking with me when
I go."

— ERMA BOMBECK

CHAPTER ONE: HISTORY OF HERBS AND SPICES

Spices and herbs have worked to flavor food and life from civilization to civilization. In the Middle East, thyme, cardamom, saffron, myrrh, and dill were grown everywhere from the royal gardens to common household gardens. Indian culture utilizes different spices and flavors used in food preparation, wellness, and worship. Ancient Greeks included garlic in most of their cooking, and they imported herbs from neighboring countries, which they used very creatively. For instance, they would wear crowns made with marjoram and parsley to ward off drunkenness during their festivals.

In Europe, early uses of herbs and spices were predominantly by the wealthy. Did you know that spices and herbs were also the currency in most previously mentioned cultures, including European, Middle Eastern, and Roman-Greek? But with time, the spices became more available on the market, and the prices dropped. Soon, people could grow them in their gardens, making homemade remedies and elixirs.

The importance of spices extended to national and international matters. In Colonial America, anyone drinking the same tea that the British drank was deemed unpatriotic. To show disdain for the British, Americans resorted to making their tea using different spices and herbs, replacing traditional tea. They used sage, chamomile flowers, lemon balm leaves, spearmint leaves, and sassafras bark, among others, for their tea. The next time you reach for your sage tea or chamomile tea before bed, thank those early Americans for their intense dislike of the British during colonialism.

Then spices finally arrived in America as the trade route extended from Asia to Europe. By that time, the Asian continent had already begun enjoying the benefits of the trade. The European continent was yet to see an uptake in the spice industry. However, Mediterranean countries had the monopoly of spice trade and production. Arab merchants would load their caravans and journey through China and India, trading with local merchants for leather products, ebony, precious stones, and gold.

Others discovered herbs and spices quite by default. Hunters and fishing communities found that their meat becomes flavored when they wrap their catch of the day in particular leaves. The Romans would spice their wine to enhance the taste. They also placed some of the herbs and spices in their lotions and bath oils to scent their bodies. As a result, we inherited from our forefathers' knowledge of utilizing spices to make our food healthier and tastier. Herbs have now become a way of life for people of all walks of life. In this book, we will explore the uses of spices.

According to health professionals, the amount of preservatives in many of the foods we enjoy is very unhealthy. You can use spices and herbs to flavor the food limiting the use of salts and sugars that can be extremely harmful. Herbs contain most of the vitamins and nutrients we need, as demonstrated by a simple bay leaf.

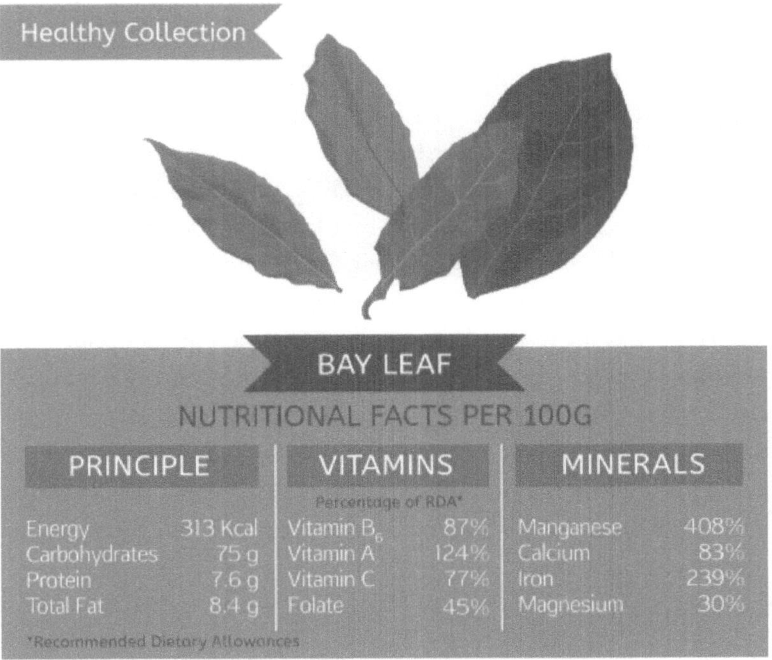

THE OLDEST SPICES IN THE WORLD

Peppercorn

Pepper is almost synonymous with cooking and taste enhancement of food. Look at your recipe book or watch any cooking show, and the pepper is present most of the time. It could be due to how long it has been with us or how well it has served humanity over the years. Whatever it is, it remains one of the most common spices in all kitchens around the world.

In the culinary world, black pepper is the "flavor of Kerala." It is one of the oldest spices in the world. It is the source of the typical black pepper and comes from small berries. They harvest these berries when they are red, which means they are mature. They then boil the red peppercorns until they turn black, and then dry and grind them to a powder.

Today peppercorn is grown all over the tropics, but it is native to Southern India. It has been present in Indian cultures at least as far back as 2000 BC, and it is one of the spices that India exported in large quantities. It was so widely traded that peppercorn trade evidence has been found in Egyptian merchant scrolls and even in the nostrils of Ramses, an Egyptian Pharaoh. In ancient Rome, the spice was in 80% of the meals. However, the Arabs soon became dominant players in the black pepper trade when the Roman empire fell, spreading the spice through the Indian Ocean and China's southern coast.

There was a myth spread by the Arab merchants about how precious the mystic black pepper was. The legend said that venomous snakes guarded the peppercorn groves in India. Burning the trees was necessary to kill and drive the serpents away, leaving the peppercorn fruit black. This myth was effective in increasing the prices since the spice was considered even more precious.

Saffron

Have you checked the price of saffron lately? You can rest assured that the store was not trying to get more money from your pocket. The price is that high everywhere in the world and has been for ages. Saffron takes the cup for the world's most expensive spice and is among the oldest. Please do not feel so bad that it is not in your pantry, although you should buy it once for the taste test.

Saffron comes from the flower Crocus sativus, which can't grow in the wild. Since it requires human intervention and growth methods, it is a labor-intensive crop, which drives up the price. Nurturing a healthy crop of saffron is painstaking, and it is picked only by hand. The specific part of the plant used is the orange-red stigmas of the flowers. Farmers harvest these on the morning that they bloom.

Saffron thrives in dry, sunny areas. Iran is the world's largest producer of the spice. Farmers in the region have been growing it for centuries. But generations of saffron farmers in Iran don't even scratch the surface of the history of saffron. Cleopatra used this age-old spice to prepare her skin when she had suitors calling. In Persia, it was present during deity worship, and they also spread strands on their beds to cure melancholy. The Persian Pilau features the rich glowing yellow punch of saffron, while Spanish cuisine uses the spice liberally in their paella, stews, desserts, and baked goods.

Minoan ladies used saffron dye on their bolero jackets and also to make lipstick by adding it into beeswax, red ochre, and tallo. During the bubonic plague, the spice was prescribed by some as an antidote. The great thing with saffron is that a little bit goes a long way.

There is an ancient Greek legend surrounding saffron detailing a love story of Smilax and Crocus. Crocus, a handsome young man, goes looking for a beautiful nymph by the name of Smilax. He finds her in the woods near Athens, and they spend a brief but idyllic period of love. In the beginning, she is flattered by his amorous proclamations and pursuit. However, she tires of him, but he is still in love with her. She becomes angry at his advances, which continue even after telling him it is over. So she bewitches him, transforming him into a saffron crocus flower, and the bright red orange-red stigmas are a lasting symbol of the passion he still carries for Smilax.

Saffron only blooms once a year and only for one week in the year.

· · ·

Turmeric

Turmeric features a beautiful yellow glow. This hue has earned it the name the Golden spice and, in some cases, "the Indian saffron." Turmeric is traceable to 5000 years in India, where it featured heavily in their Vedic culture. Here it was not only used in cooking but also religious ceremonies. In the Hindu religion, turmeric's yellowish/orange color represents the meeting of purity, sensuality, fertility, and prosperity.

The spice was also for medicinal uses, thanks to the presence of curcumin. Curcumin has anti-inflammatory properties, which make it as efficient as ibuprofen. The same substance also provides the spice with a rich yellow color. The botanical name of turmeric is Curcuma longa.

The yellow-orange hue of turmeric dyes threads and clothing. The dyed materials make the robes of Buddhist monks and children's clothing during the Kerala Onam festival. In an Indian wedding, the groom drapes the bride with turmeric dyed yellow strings around the neck to signify that she is married and can handle wifely duties. The necklace is known as the Mangalsutra, and to date, it is still prevalent in the Hindu community. It is equivalent to the exchange of rings.

They also put turmeric in poultices to cure skin conditions while inhaling fumes from burning turmeric. Before long, the spice reached China via their southern coast, East Africa via the Indian Ocean, and the Caribbean via the Caribbean sea. Arab traders were the leading turmeric traders, with the colonial Europeans eventually bringing the spice into Europe. Once the spice made its way into the European continent, we saw the infamous curry powder's emergence. Curry powder contains lots of turmeric. Turmeric belongs to the ginger family, and that explains why it is excellent when combined with ginger.

· · ·

Cardamom

This spice is another close relative to ginger, but it comes from the plant's seeds rather than the root. The seeds are dried and cured before being crushed to form the spice. Cardamom is popular because of its intense aroma, which smells like ginger and cinnamon combined. It is a loved spice in both Indian and Middle Eastern cultures. In these cultures it has a history of over 4000 years, especially in their cuisine. The Egyptians mixed it in their embalming spices to use on their mummies.

Greeks and Romans loved the spice's scent in their lotions, balms, oils, and perfume. However, the moors became the most impacted by this spice and made it a staple in their dishes. Scandinavians are second to Arabs in their love for cardamom. Countries like Sweden and Norway consume almost thirty times more cardamom per capita compared to other countries.

The Vikings brought cardamom into their countries because of extensive trading with the Turkish merchants in the Byzantine empire. They also had access to the spice when it reached regions like Cologne in Germany because of trade with the Moors.

Southern India is the native home for cardamom, where it grows in the wild. Being one of the world's most ancient spices, it has quite a following in making beverages and baked goods. It also features in dishes like rice and meat stews. There are three types of cardamom: black, green, and Madagascar cardamom. Green cardamom is expensive because it packs a lot of flavor. It is best to buy any cardamom while it is still in its pods and grind it as you need to use. Ground cardamom loses its flavor, so storing it while ground means that you are losing its aroma and taste with time.

Cinnamon

Can you believe that at one point, cinnamon was more expensive than gold. It was the currency of choice when merchants were trading in spices. There are few things as decadent as walking into a kitchen or bakery where cinnamon features in the food. This spice is native to Sri Lanka, and its botanical name is Cinnamomum zeylanicum.

Ancient Egyptians also used cinnamon in their embalming process. This old spice was very much a part of the Egyptian culture, and with good reason; It could change the scent of a room or a person instantly. This spice was also in Chinese civilization. It is known as Kwai in Cantonese. The Hebrews and Arabs called it Amomon, and the Romans referred to it as Cinnamomum.

Cinnamon is the bark of the Cinnamomum verum tree. It is also native to other countries like China, Burma, and Vietnam. In medieval times the physicians used this spice to treat respiratory illnesses like sore throats and coughs. It was useful in preserving meats in different cultures because it contains phenols that prevent bacteria that cause rot in meat. The Dutch, through the Dutch East India Company, had the monopoly of the cinnamon trade. However, once it could grow all over the world from Mauritius to South America, there was no more monopoly.

Cloves

Cloves were traceable to Indonesia in the 8th century. The first references to cloves were in Han Oriental literature, but the spice soon became synonymous with European trade and commerce. The clove forests in the Molucca islands of Indonesia were so enchantingly fragrant and evergreen. The trees' presence is attributable to the parents' custom of planting a tree every time a baby was born. The tradition meant that as long as children were born, the planting of clove trees would continue, and of course, there would be trade. We should borrow that custom, not necessarily cloves, but a tree for every child. Consider that.

Aside from the birth custom, cloves were so valuable that they were the reason for wars. Well, not the clove itself but the trees. The Europeans and natives of Indonesia wanted exclusive rights to the trees, and they muscled it out. They knew that whoever was in-charge had the advantage in trading the spice. A fight ensued for trees with an intense flavor but loved by people worldwide. The spice has a penetrating flavor and taste. And it is medicinal. If you have that terrible toothache, reach out for the clove. Its numbing effect, when used in the mouth, helps to relieve tooth pain. You can utilize the spice as a whole clover or in its ground form. This spice also stabilizes blood sugar levels as well as enhancing liver health. You see why they had to fight over it, for all the health benefits. That's not entirely true. The focus here was on the trade.

Star anise

This spice has an iconic flavor in a star, not the one in our skies, but a star-shaped pod. Star Anise is native to China and Vietnam, and it grows on an evergreen tree. Some people refer to it as the Chinese star spice. Before coming to Europe in the 16-17th centuries, it was used by the Chinese and Vietnamese cultures as far back as 100 B.C. It has a distinct licorice flavor making it popular in jams and other compotes once it hit the European market. This spice found its way to Europe courtesy of an English sailor who took it back home from his Far East travels.

Star anise is the seed pod of the Illicium verum plant. It must not be confused with Spanish anise, which also features the licorice flavor. The plants are not related, but both contain anethole, the compound responsible for the taste. This spice is rich in antioxidants as well as vitamin C and A. Oil derived from star anise contains thymol and terpineol, which help treat coughs and touches of flu—something we all need during the flu season. Farmers harvest the fruits containing the star-shaped seed pods right before they mature and dry completely in the sun. You can use the pod as it is by dropping it into the food. This spice is synonymous with Asian dishes like marbled eggs and Pho.

. . .

Allspice

Many people take Allspice to be a mixture of a good number of spices, if not all. That is far from the truth. Allspice is an independent, powerful spice whose only relation to others is her smell. She does have a combination of different aromas that earned her the name. More like the traditional woman smells of food, soap, milk, manure, perfume, and even dust from all the cleaning. Similarly, Allspice smells of nutmeg, cinnamon, pepper, and cloves.

The discovery of Allspice was by Christopher Columbus during his travels in the Caribbean. This spice is unripe berries from the Pimenta dioica tree that have been sundried. It has an exciting amalgamation of scents ranging from nutmeg to cinnamon and cloves. It is a favorite in baked goods and also in meat dishes, especially those featuring minced meat. When Columbus and his Spanish explorers discovered this spice, they first mistook it for black pepper, Pimienta. It soon proved to be different and invaluable to their cuisine and has remained a popular option since then. But the mixup is understandable because Allspice looks like a black peppercorn. It is available in countries like Jamaica, Honduras, and Guatemala, among others, and it still retains the name, Pimienta.

Often, it is confused with the Chinese five-spice. Chinese five-spice is a mixture of five different spices: star anise, cinnamon, cloves, Szechwan, and fennel. Allspice is one spice that has elements of different scents occurring naturally. This spice grows exclusively in the western hemisphere.

"The Romans brought with them spices such as ginger, pepper and cinnamon, and herbs including borage, chervil, dill, fennel, lovage, sage and thyme, all of which have remained staples of the British kitchen."

— MONTY DON

S affron: The spice of royalty

There is a small part of each of us that leans towards royalty, either the crowns or by association. You see how people want to take photos with presidents and those in power. Let's talk about power; we all want it, the better if it came with no responsibilities. Too bad, they come together. We also want money, lots of it. There was a time when spices held all that. Take Saffron, for instance; having it was and still is a sign of doing well financially.

Have you ever noted how nature is abundant in medicine? When the black plague began in western Europe, healers and physicians turned to spices and herbs to find a cure. Behaviors changed, including in spices like cassia, ginger, cinnamon, and cloves instead of plain water. Of course, the wealthy were the first to benefit and carried pouches with spices like black pepper, turmeric, garlic, cardamom, and cloves as medication. Monasteries also used cinnamon, pepper, and crushed snails to treat headaches and insomnia. Herbal medicine has been part of the most ancient civilizations in the European continent and with significant results.

In the middle ages, spices and herbs were precious commodities that were expensive and highly regarded. Even in medieval times, there was a high demand for flavored foods. In many ways, spices and herbs were the pathways for global trading and economic networks and, unfortunately, for conquest, war, and exploitation.

The aggressive exploration of spices and herbs was due to the limited supply, high demand, and mysterious origins. Of course, the high, mighty, and wealthy got the first share. In the 14th century, spices like long pepper and grains of paradise could be found in the marketplace even though they are native to India and West Africa.

EUROPEAN NOBILITY AND HERBS AND SPICES

The truth is that spices and herbs were already a global commodity even before European voyages began. However, their desire to control the trade led to military excursions that fueled colonial empires, giving them commercial superiority on the global scene. It also led to creating the influential Dutch company, which dominated the spice trade in Europe. From the papacy to the rulers of Cyprus and wealthy merchants of Genoa and Venice, there were very many vested interests in the spice trade. These interests promoted the practice of exploitation from the local markets to the sources of the spices.

On the European continent, spices were costly because European merchants convinced themselves and their buyers that the herbs were rare. They became a symbol of status for the wealthy, and also, they were medicinal. Besides, when the Roman empire fell, wars erupted worldwide, cutting off trade routes for spices and making accessibility harder for spice merchants.

Marauding religious crusaders tasted the middle eastern spices in Roman cuisine, which piqued their interest in the flavors—consequently bringing the use of herbs and spices back home to their nobles. As a result, nobles became an integral customer base for the spice traders.

Even though the West was a dominant player in trade and use, they eventually adopted an unfavorable view of different flavors that saw spices almost entirely omitted from their dishes. That is because since Europe controlled a lot of spice routes, spices became more available in Europe and less exclusive. The law of demand; the higher the supply, the lower the market. By losing their exclusivity, spices became less appealing for nobles. They also became less of a status symbol. When the wealthy recoiled from using spices in their dishes because it was available in less affluent households, they reverted to unspiced meals.

The nobles decided that they will "allow" foods to retain their natural taste. For example, meat was to remain unspiced so that the beef or venison tastes has the animal's natural flavor. And with this decision came the gradual but sure decline in uses of spices in Europe's noble households. Also, it came with the fall of the power and value of spices. This shift in the use of spices and herbs began in France and soon spread throughout Europe.

Medically, the same happened as the wealthy were unwilling

to be treated using herbal medicines like everyone else. Apoc-athiries were for the local population and advanced medical techniques by personal physicians for the wealthy and noble families. Soon enough, spices and herbs lost meaning and value even to the local people who always followed their nobles' trends.

AFRICAN KINGS AND QUEENS USE OF HERBS AND SPICES

From Amina, the warrior queen of Hausaland, to Cleopatra, queen of Egypt, African Kings and queens have had a healthy reverence for herbs. It took a bit longer before spices lost their value in Africa, Asia, and the Middle East. For example, Queen Amina expanded the borders of Hausaland, modern-day North-east Nigeria. She also traded in exotic goods, including kola nuts, salt, and seeds. Her trading prowess brought some of the herbs that became popular with their local healers known as bokaye. The bokaye would also be a farmer who grew his/her own medicine. They would use the herbs to treat ailments ranging from respiratory illnesses to skin conditions and wounds from wars.

Queen Amina's control of the vast region guaranteed Arab traders safe passage through the Sahara region, and in return, they traded some spices favorably with the people. For example, they sold mint, which locally became known as Naana. Locally their cuisine had the hot west African pepper, which they used to flavor their meats and vegetable stews. As the Arabs traveled, they continued to grow the lucrative spices trade everywhere they went.

Waging wars was common for Kings and queens to expand their territories, so they needed herbal medicine for their wounded soldiers. There were a few exceptions, like Cleopatra, who used herbs for personal care and beauty. Cleopatra was a beauty and a femme fatale. All of this was possible because of spices/herbs and, of course, the interventions of the gods.

Other African kings and queens used herbs and traditional healers in medicine and sacred rituals. For example, in the times of Shaka Zulu, his people, including the army, believed in the sangoma's healing powers, both divine and physical, using herbs.

The royal groups in Congo also used herbs and medicine collected from the vast Congo forest. In fact, until this day, most Congolese believe each man is a doctor because of herbal plants' easy availability. Nature has it all.

In the story about King Solomon and Queen Sheba, the

queen was a ruler of a vast region, including Ethiopia. On her journey to test the king on his wisdom, she brings him spices and gold, which she gifts him after realizing his judgment is beyond reproach. All the above examples show how revered herbs and spice were in African kingdoms for medical purposes and currency.

Apart from the rulers, individual tribes traded in spices, making them influential players in the spice trade. For centuries, the Tuareg tribe from the West African Sahara dealt in ivory, jewelry, and spices, with their most considerable profits from the spice trade. Tuareg is the Arabic word for "abandoned by God," but the tribe also calls themselves Imohad, which means "free men." With their ancestry steeped in the Berber of North Africa, these African peoples are nomads, so they traveled far and wide to trade with others and to look for pasture for their animals.

Known as the Lords of the Sahara, they are famous for their caravans of salt, which brought salt to various corners of the globe and spices like cardamom and grains of paradise. The most notable Tuareg trade trail was the Taghaza Trail, which began from the town of Aoudaghost near the city of Fez in Morocco and worked its way down to what is modern-day Freetown in Sierra Leone, passing through Bamako, Ghana.

The West African rulers especially favored the spices that augured well with local cuisine like the hot peppers. They believed the hot peppers gave them the vitality and strength needed to rule their people.

On this trade route, they traded in saffron, dates, and oil lamps, among other things. They also had different trade routes towards the north ending in Egypt, where they brought items like cowrie shells, gold, ebony, ivory slaves, and yes, some saffron. In exchange, they got spices like fennel, myrrh, frankincense, and cumin, which they traded along the way back home. Some of the popular herbs sold under the rule of famous African kings and queens include Guinea pepper - grains of paradise, African blue basil, African negro pepper, Cumin, Garlic, Ginger, Jamaican nutmeg, Berbere spice

It is interesting to learn that Egyptian civilization was not only focused on pyramid building. There were advanced techniques to medicine, cosmetic preparation, and afterlife preparations because the pharaohs were committed to luxury in this life and the next. In ancient Egypt, the pharaohs were both god and man, so their approach to illness was a fight between good and evil. The sickness was considered a reproach from the gods. Priests and healers were to work on a tandem solution. The priests gave offerings to the gods, while the healers used herbs and spices to get a physical cure. In this way, physical medicine complemented mystical solutions.

Egyptian healers were ahead of their times, especially in their knowledge of human anatomy and how different herbs interact with the body. They used all manner of medicines from opium, myrrh, fennel, and frankincense to cannabis, thyme, and aloe to take care of skin conditions, respiratory illnesses, and digestive issues. The pharaohs regularly took garlic and onion, which the healers believed aided in endurance. They steeped the herbs in wine, drank the concoction or peeled cloves, crushed them, and mixed them in vinegar to use a mouth wash.

Egyptian nobility, under the instruction of healers and priests, would wear freshly peeled cloves of raw garlic wrapped in cheesecloth or muslin in their undergarments to protect themselves against diseases like flu and the common cold. The palace trusted the personal physicians of the Pharaohs to make various herbal medicines, effective concoctions, and poultices to heal royal ailments.

Egypt's proximity to the Nile meant that the people, pharaohs included, suffered from repeated bouts of malaria. King Tut was one of the pharaohs who was uniquely afflicted by the disease because of his weak immunity. Royal healers would make herbal concoctions using ginger, garlic, herbs, and spices to reduce fever and cure the disease.

But perhaps the most significant proof of the use of herbs in ancient Egyptian civilization is herbs and spices in the mummy remains of pharaohs. The detailed mummification process used on Egyptian mummies of royalty has helped modern-day science understand their features and existing ailments.

The embalming, with its spices and herbs, preserved the DNA of the dead royal family members. That gave scientists insight into the family relationship between the pharaohs they found buried hundreds of years ago.

Today, many scientists praise the herbs' active mummification properties because they preserved the information about ancient pharaohs from Egypt. Egyptians would remove the dead pharaoh's internal organs, steep them in incense infused sweetened wine, dehydrate them in a saline solution, and cover them with hot gum resin. After this, they would place them in urns ready for burial with the body.

Cleaning the body was with herbs with a high aromatic value like cinnamon, cloves, myrrh, anise, and cumin. The next step would be stuffing it with dehydrating plants that removed the body's moisture and retained the form. For the next 40-70 days, they would soak the body in a solution that dissolved the body fat. When they removed the body from this solution, they would wash it, dry it, and coat the internal cavities with hot resin. Afterward, they would stuff the body permanently with aromatic herbs and spices.

Once again, the body was waxed, coated with cedar gum and oil, and you guessed right: aromatic spices and herbs. Some herbs were exclusive to Egyptian royalty embalming, including:

Myrrh: This herb was crucial for the embalming process. It is available in powdered form or as crystals. They also burned it as incense to repel insects from the embalming temples.

Anise: Anise oil was popular for its antiseptic properties.

Frankincense: This herb stuffed the corpse's inside cavity after they had removed the internal organs.

Cumin: Cumin was instrumental in killing the bacteria during the embalming process.

Other spices like fennel and cloves had aromatic value and were necessary during the dead's sacred rituals.

MEXICO, CENTRAL AND SOUTH AMERICA NOBILITY

Although the Central and South American countries and cultures used herbs and spices to flavor their food, they were inept as traders when using spices as currency. For example, in the pre-Columbian Aztec culture, the Aztec nobility used vanilla to flavor their beverages and wore the pods around their necks to perfume their bodies.

However, it took the Dutch, British and French smuggling the plant of the Portuguese and Spanish colonies to grow it for large-scale reproduction and trade. They found a way to hand pollinate the plants allowing them to spread the plant in the spice trade. The Portuguese also took spices and herbs like the Brazilian hot peppers around the world to trade them. In most South American applications, the hottest varieties were medicine and insect repellent. They also used them in their weapons against marauding Spanish soldiers. There were little to no spice trade routes into the Americas.

INDIAN ROYALTY

Britain's fight to control India was because the westerners wanted to control the spice trade in the country. However, unlike the rest of the world that viewed spices as money, as a preserve of some people, and a precious commodity, the Indians held a genuine love and appreciation for them, they still do. The spices were all sold in local markets visited by both the local population and royal families. Their use of herbs, particularly for medicinal purposes, was extensive and open to all.

In the Indian way of life, ayurvedic medicine featured prominently, and it used the knowledge of the plants and the understanding of human anatomy to heal and promote wellness. In applying ayurvedic herbs for healing, the Indian healers worked to purify the patient's blood, restore normal functions into place, and expel foreign or offensive elements. As a result, the medicines used were diuretics, fever and pain relievers, immunity boosters, inflammation medicines, and aphrodisiacs. The exciting thing with spices and herbs in the Indian culture is that they appear equally across the regions. That allowed everyone to enjoy the same level of wellness and health.

The most important spices for an Indian household (and the royal palace) include:

Tulsi: The people also know this Indian herb as the "Queen of the herbs." It grows all over, and it was ever-present in the royal gardens. It was in place to keep the atmosphere around the palace pure.

Cardamom: The seed from this plant is both sweet and lemony. It is the most popular spice in India used in sweets and desserts.

Chiles: Indian cuisine in the royal household was not complete without chiles. These are roasted, fried, and served as a side dish for rice.

Turmeric: Turmeric is synonymous with Indian curries and other Indian foods. It is common in their beverages and desserts.

Fennel seeds: Indians eat fennel seeds before they sit down for their meals to help with indigestion.

CHINESE ROYALTY

Legendary Chinese emperor Huang Ti, also known as the yellow emperor, was one of traditional Chinese medicine's first reference points (TCM). His writings helped modern scientists understand that rulers had a special relationship with healing and medicine in TCM. It was divine and physical at the same time.

Sheng Nung is another Chinese emperor who valued plants. He participated in divine farming, meaning that the emperor planted medicinal plants, which he tasted himself before he used them on anyone else. He was revered as a healer and known as the Father of Chinese medicine. He also created the technique of acupuncture. Other great wealthy physicians existed in the Han and Ming dynasties. Chang Chung Ching was one of the most influential Chinese medicine figures, earning the name Hippocrate of China.

With time the Chinese herbs became popular in the global spice trade. In the Chinese spice trade, maritime routes were crucial. These routes convoyed the spices from the Chinese shores to other parts of the world, and they carried spices like saffron, cinnamon, and ginger, among others. The routes were the spice roads or silk roads, and they extended to other spice islands like the Molucca islands in Indonesia.

The silk roads were dangerous, which added to the value and allure of merchants' traded spices. There were bandits and pirates, not to mention the heat of the desert, harsh mountain terrain, and wild animals. The silk road started during the Han dynasty, and they were a series of routes that led from China to Rome. However, spices were not the only intriguing thing to come out of China. The Romans had been looking for sources of the silk they got during their conquests, and with the silk road, they finally found the "silk people."

Three main routes brought significant interaction and growth of the spice trade for the Chinese people. The central route ran from China, west through Persia, and the Mediterranean sea and then to Rome; The northern route came from China through the Black Sea and Rome. Finally, the Southern route ran from China to Iran into India.

The Chinese boats used in the trade of spices and silk were small and faced many perils on the high seas. They were junk boats used by both Chinese and Korean traders. So in most cases, they would trade with the Arabs on the high seas, and once the trading was over, they would turn back. With time they learned shipbuilding from the Arabs, who had larger and more superior vessels, and they began to transport their goods to the final destination.

MIDDLE EAST AND TURKEY POWERS

The Middle East and Turkey (part of ancient Mesopotamia) prominently feature in the spice trade and the growth of the love of spices worldwide. Mesopotamia extended to Iraq, and this part of the world has some of the most flavor-packed cuisines because of herbs and spices.

The King of Babylon, Merodach-Baladan II, had an extensive array of spices in his royal garden, including garlic, cardamom, turmeric, saffron, coriander, and thyme. That meant that he had culinary herbs in his backyard and his natural medicine chest to heal his family members when they fell ill.

Interestingly, the Arabic and Muslim cultures are very invested in using herbs and spices to enhance the dish's flavor. But spices in the Arabic culture were more than just food flavorings. They were hard currency. Unbelievably, you could buy a slave's freedom using spices like 500 grams of black pepper. Spice traders were extraordinarily wealthy and wielded a lot of power in the Arabian Peninsula. Centuries long gone saw the Arabic merchants build a reputation as renowned sellers of various spices like nutmeg, ginger, cinnamon, cardamom, and pepper. They sold in places like Venice, where they made their way into the rest of Europe.

Soon enough, the West wanted complete control of the spices and their trade routes, which were dominated by the Arabs. European colonialists and traders didn't want to deal with non-christian powers who ran the lucrative spice trade. That led to the battles and then full-blown crusade wars with religious and political interests and economic reasons. Europe began to trade significantly in spices and herbs during the crusades because the fighting weakened the Muslim hold on the lucrative trade routes.

However, Arab spice traders' networks extended far and wide from the Middle East to North Africa and Asia. The networks were so advanced that even when Europe became apathetic to herbs and spices, the Arab spice trade continued, and it still thrived.

For centuries spices and herbs ruled the world from one corner of the earth to the other. Christopher Columbus captured the mentality behind the power and value of spices with this quote:

> *"But in truth, should I meet with gold or spices in great quantity, I shall remain till I collect as much as possible, and for this purpose I am proceeding solely in quest of them."*

> — *CHRISTOPHER COLUMBUS*

CHAPTER THREE: HEALING FROM THE PAST

Herbs and spices have been used since time immemorial to aid in healing the body. From healing Shamans to Roman and Greek healers, there is ample proof of herbs and spices' use in making people feel better. Simple tonics proved to be effective when used with the correct ailment. So how did humanity use herbs and spices in healing?

YOGIS' USE

Herbs are synonymous with yoga because traditionally, there have been specific yogic herbs accompanying the practice. Herbs aid in awakening our higher faculties and increasing vitality. Traditional yogis will ingest the herbs in small quantities to create subtle natural changes to the nervous system and perception. The herbs' effects are not to be confused with the psychedelic effect of recreational drugs like cannabis Sativa.

In traditional yoga, there is the use of herbs like Ashwagandha, Amalaki, and haritaki. Ashwagandha is excellent at helping you adapt to stress by controlling your levels of anxiety. That is in addition to boosting brain function and lowering blood sugar.

Amalaki is excellent for detoxing the body and also sharpening the memory. Haritaki is known for maintaining overall health with its anti-inflammatory properties. Herbs like Haritaki have, for thousands of years, been available in ayurvedic medicine and yoga meditation. These herbs catalyze yogi processes, which we can't achieve by personal effort alone.

There is a place for common spices like cinnamon, ginger, and turmeric, which helps you remain in your healthiest form for yogic processes. For yogis, ginger will increase Agni (digestive fire) throughout the body, while turmeric relieves joint pain for flexibility during yoga poses. Turmeric also has a powerful effect on the mood and ability to concentrate because the curcumin in it boosts your levels of dopamine.

GREECE AND THE ROMAN EMPIRE USE OF SPICES FOR HEALING

Alexander the Great's conquests were instrumental in bringing a lot of medicinal spices to the Greek shores. And from there, it was easy for the same spices to make it to Rome. Ancient Greek and Roman medicine were among the most advanced of its time, mainly because of herbs and spices. Both civilizations were in continuous warfare, creating a need for advanced medical knowledge to treat their soldiers.

You can say their knowledge of medicinal herbs and spices was out of necessity. The use of these herbs was practical in Rome and Greece compared to Babylon and Egypt, where they were considered magical. In cosmetics, their purpose was reversing aging. The wealthy Romans and Greeks were obsessed with youth and looking excellent, leading to herbal pursuits to stem aging. Each Greek/Roman household had a small garden where they grew the most common spices. For the more exotic herbs and spices, they went to the marketplace. Some of the popular herbs used during this time include:

Charlock: This herb is also known as Brassica, and it was one of the most valued medicinal plants in Rome. The Latin name for the herb is Sinapis arvensis, and its use was to overcome "melancholia" or "the gloom." The Romans and Greeks ate the leaves in their salads when the young shoots and leaves came in the spring. They cooked Charlock flowers, and the seeds, which have a hot mustard flavor, were dried and ground into a powder and used for flavoring. The powder was present in their most sophisticated dishes.

Lavender: If you wanted sophistication, then you went for lavender. Unlike now, when lavender is one among many scents, it was a preserve of the elite. A whole fresh flower was present in clothes drawers, and its oil in perfumes and balms.

Its Latin name Lavandula comes from the Latin verb lavare, which means to wash. Lavender was also used to heal wounds and to fight insomnia. The pain-relieving qualities of lavender were handy to Roman and Greek healers.

They used it for poultices to treat skin conditions and as an antiseptic when cleaning the soldiers' wounds. Lavender infused water was commonly for cleansing wounds. The antibacterial and antiviral properties of lavender prevented infections of the open wounds. Lavender was also used by washing women for hire to scent the clothes of their clients. The lingering scent helped people to sleep better because the lavender scent is very calming.

Catnip: Catnip was mainly in the food of the ancient Romans and Greeks. It helped them with indigestion, primarily because of their rich diet. Healers would use it as a sedative and also increase sweating in their patients during the treatment of fevers. They used the plant's dried leaves and flowers. Healers also recommended catnip for calming the nerves. The Latin name for catnip is Nepeta cataria.

Skirret: Known by the Latin name of Sium sisarum, is an aromatic root used as a vegetable. It is cooked similarly to parsnips. They are a cluster of bright white roots with a sweet taste and aromatic flavor. Although it is native to China, it arrived in Rome even before the Roman empire's growth. It was a favorite of the great Roman Emperor Tiberius. Skirret is excellent for helping with indigestion and also boosts the appetite.

Lemon thyme: Ancient greeks loved using this herb in their baths and their food as well. They would also place the leaves beneath their pillow to help them sleep. It wasn't uncommon for the womenfolk to give their loved ones thyme leaves to provide them with courage. The plant was also widely used in ancient Rome to offer a vibrant flavor in their cheeses and alcoholic beverages. They also used it to treat melancholy and as a topical treatment for skin conditions.

Parsley: Parsley was the treatment given to sterile men in ancient Rome and Greece. They also used it liberally to cure their hangover, which they politely referred to as the morning after-the-banquet- feeling. The Romans also gave garlands of parsley to newlywed couples to ward off evil spirits. Both cultures did not initially eat this herb because they mistook it for fool's parsley. However, with time it made its way into their repertoire of beloved edible herbs and became a local favorite.

Salvia: Salvia is known as sage, and in ancient Rome, it was used for healing ulcers, bleeding wounds and to soothe a sore throat. The Romans and the Greeks also used it for indigestion. Pliny the Elder, one of Rome's celebrated authors of their history, claimed that the herb is also a diuretic and local anesthetic. In the beginning, when they came across the herb, both the Greeks and Romans used it to preserve their meat. The Latin name for sage is Salvia meaning "to feel well."

Verbena: Once again, according to Pliny, the Elder's records, the holiest herb in ancient Rome was verbena. It was the best remedy for an iron wound because of its ability to fight infections that came with war injuries aggressively. It also helped reduce fever in delirious soldiers and helped them sleep. They also used it on their altars because priests in Rome and Greece believed it boosted their divination powers.

Hippocrates, one of the most respected Greek physicians of all time, relied mostly on plant-based medicine to treat his patients. He separated the religious-magical misconceptions about ailments from physical illness and found real herbal remedies to cure the latter. Hippocrates was born on the island of Kos in Greece, and to this day, the island is home to eight proven medicinal plants central to plant-based medicine.

These plants include the lentisk bush used to heal wounds, the juniper tree, an antiseptic/disinfectant, and the pomegranate, whose flowers treat inflammation. The rind of the pomegranate fruit is excellent for treating diarrhea and removing intestinal parasites. Other plants include myrtle to ease stomach aches and fennel for indigestion and coughs. There is also wormwood for indigestion, spearmint for stress relief and headaches, and finally, Greek sage for tonsillitis and digestion.

The infamous words of Hippocrates truly guided the Greek-Roman civilizations in their approach to herbs: "Let food be thy medicine and medicine thy food."

SHAMANS USE OF HERBS FROM AFRICA TO SOUTH AMERICA

The history of herbs and spices in South American culture has been evident for centuries. From the infamous Ayahuasca to the chacruna, South American shamans used everything from hallucinogenic plants to common medicinal plants to cure ailments in their communities. One of the treasured experiences in these shamans' healing rituals was using a hallucinogenic plant to induce passage into their spirit world.

This plant is still known as the teacher plant, and in places like Peru, even the government recognizes the plant as a "pillar of the Amazon people's identity." Traditional Amazonian medicine centers around the teacher plant, which is commonly known as the Ayahuasca. There is even Ayahuasca tourism, where tourists travel to Peru to consume this specific herbal medicine as part of their experience.

This medicine treats some people with post-traumatic stress disorder and recurring addictions. Expert botanists will tell you that this plant is not to be used for thrill-seeking as it doesn't have fun effects. It puts your body through emotional and physical rollercoasters. It can cause disorientation, some people throw up, and others have vivid memories come to life. However, the aftereffect is peaceful and healing.

In centuries past, shamans used this medicine to treat stomach issues as it made people vomit, removing any offensive items in their digestive system. It also helped with indigestion. Mentally the drug gave sharp focus to some users after consuming it, so some warriors used it. Nowadays, it is useful in assisting people to gain introspection, which ultimately enhances their personal development.

Ayahuasca is the most popular medicinal herb synonymous with South America for obvious reasons. However, other herbs were prominent in the shaman's hut for healing purposes.

Mugwort: Mugwort, also known as sailor's tobacco or felon weed, was used as a diuretic and even during childbirth to help women expel the afterbirth if it didn't come out naturally. Shamans also used it to sedate their patients and treat the common cold, cough, and fevers. They burnt it during their sacred rituals to purify the community and their patients before leaving the treatment hut.

Plantago Major: Another primary herb popular with South American shamans was the Plantago major known as the snakebite or rat's tail. This herb was instrumental in treating stings and insect bites, a common occurrence in the Amazon forest. The roots and leaves were useful in treating urinary tract infections and hemorrhoids. The juice was beneficial topically to heal sores, ringworms, boils, and soothe inflammations. Shamans ground the seeds and gave them orally to help stimulate internal healing.

Watercress: They also used watercress for colds and coughs. Watercress is rich in vitamin C, which explains why it was such a useful herb for curing colds. The leaves are edible, and shamans mixed them with wild honey to make a concoction for their patients. Sometimes they would ask the patient to place the leaves under their tongue and leave it there. The leaves have a peppery flavor and induce a slight burning sensation. By breathing through the leaves, they release heat that can help with respiratory ailments.

Viper's bugloss: This was also common in the healer's repertoire of medicines. It helped them manage patient's fevers and also provided pain relief in snakebites. Patients with coughs found this herb to be an excellent expectorant, and it also helped with melancholy. Shamans would also recommend the herb for people to keep away snakes.

Chamomile: Chamomile treats burns and helps induce calmness and sleep in patients. It was used topically by shamans for healing skin conditions, and they would also give it to patients to eat the flowers. Because it is a gentle herb, it was also available for babies to help with colic.

AFRICAN SHAMANS

Traditional medicines still make up a large part of the healing systems in Africa. According to WHO, some countries have up to 90% of their population relying on herbs as their primary health care. The World Health Organization has encouraged African governments to integrate traditional medical practices into their health systems.

By far, African traditional medicine is the most assorted and perhaps the oldest form of herbal medicine system. The approach to herbal medicine on the continent is both holistic and physical. The sustained use of herbal medicine in Africa is partly because of a lack of continued access to western medicine and a disproportionate spread of disease in Africa than other parts of the world.

Names given to African healers include Inyanga and Sangoma in southern Africa, Bokomowo in Ghana, Dibia in Nigeria, Laibon in Kenya, Mganga in Tanzania, and Mugwenu in Zambia.

The herbs that were a regular part of the African healer's medicine chest include:

Acacia Senegal: This herb was useful for coughs and colds, diarrhea, typhoid fever, and to curb infections on wounds. Its strong antimicrobial properties made it the go-to medicine for any respiratory disease. And since it is not toxic to the human body, it was applicable for both children and adults.

Wormwood: This is an aromatic shrub that occurs mainly in Northern Africa. It was primarily used by the Berbers of Morocco, who treated stomach disorders as well as diarrhea. They used the juice extracted from the barks or leaves of the plant. The leaves have strong antifungal properties, making them an effective treatment of beard ringworms.

Rooibos: This herb is popular in Southern Africa, treating stomach cramps and colic in babies. The healers made a drink for the patient, and for children, it was added to their milk or given in tiny sips to breastfeeding babies. It was also available for pregnant women to keep them healthy, and it later turns out that it helped with gestational hypertension in pregnancy.

Centella: Madagascar excelled in this herb's use and trade as they sold it to Arab traders. Their medicine men and women used it to heal all manner of skin diseases from leprosy to ringworms. They also gave it to patients to break fevers, help soothe inflammation, treat syphilis, and aid with diarrhea. It was useful for patients who had rheumatism with excellent results.

Madagascan Periwinkle: The healers used this herb in Madagascar to treat skin disorders and venereal diseases. They used the leaves, petals from the flowers, stems, and seeds to make a poultice applied to the area. It has high amounts of antioxidants that help with cell regeneration.

Devil's claw: This herb is native to Botswana and Namibia's red sand regions and was used extensively by the Khoi and San people of the Kalahari. The healers used it during childbirth to ease the mother's pain and on the skin for boils and other skin conditions. It also relieves fevers, headaches, back and joint pain, heartburn and indigestion, malaria, and as a sedative in some cases. It was effective in treating urinary tract infections and sores as well.

The approach of herbal medicine in Africa has always been that both western medicine and herbs can exist in the same space while complementing each other's efforts. Where newer diseases like HIV/AIDS emerged, herbalists knew they couldn't treat the condition. Still, they continued to offer herbs that can help with opportunistic infections like TB, venereal diseases, and thrush.

On top of using herbs to heal the body, some spices were essential in sacred places and rituals. For example, the Sout h African sangomas were also divine leaders, and they used herbs during some of their divination rituals. Sometimes a diagnosis of the specific disease that one was suffering from was through spiritual means using the herbs to summon healing spirits.

NORTH AMERICAN MEDICINE MEN/WOMEN AND HEALERS

Indigenous native Americans had their pulse on what nature had to offer to get their bodies functioning at optimum. Herbal use promoted mental acuity seeing as they were hunter-gatherers. Their well being is close to the earth, so they strove, and strive to live in harmony with their environment.

This culture understood that without the plants around them, they would perish. Herbs were the first defense for their Shamans, who used them for sacred rituals and to heal community members. Name it; there was something for everything they encountered, from a rattlesnake bite to the setting of broken bones. Sedatives and poultices for the skin were available right outside the teepees. Some of the herbs used by North American shamans include:

American berry cramp bark: This herb is a diuretic, and it can relieve spasms and cramps. It also worked effectively in reducing fever and flu symptoms. The shaman recommended this plant for patients suffering from eczema. They used the bark of the tree to make their medicines.

American elder: This was their pain and fever reliever used for anything from headaches to influenza. Seeing as they endured very harsh winters, they needed something for the flu season, which worked for this purpose.

Arnica: This herb also acted as a pain reliever, primarily prescribed for community members who suffered from chronic backaches. It was applicable in fighting infections from wounds and aiding in healing. Some shamans used it as a topical application on bruises, arthritic joints, and minor skin irritations.

American linden: When people came to the shamans with stomach aches and indigestion, American linden was the first medical option. Considering the diet of the native Americans consisted mainly of meat, indigestion was a common condition. It was also effective in treating headaches and fever. The healers used it for people with the common cold because the cold came with headaches and fever.

Flowering dogwood: This herb was useful in poultices for the skin and wounds. Shamans also found it to be effective against pneumonia and severe fevers. They made ointment out of the inner bark and berries of this plant. These parts of the tree have the most concentration of potency needed.

Gum plant: This was another excellent way to treat cases of flu, coughs, and colds. They also used it to help with poor digestion. Taking it before eating to help activate the digestive juices and set the stage for easy digestion. It was also helpful during the cold seasons as it aided the community to beat respiratory illnesses synonymous with the brutal winters of the mountainous regions of southwest America.

CHINESE MEDICINE

Chinese use of herbal medicine dates back to over 2,000 years ago. There are written records from the Yellow Emperor's classic excerpts that clearly show how herbs and spices were useful to heal diseases. In addition to herbs' use, the Chinese culture loves using acupuncture to identify regions in the body that would aid in the healing process with a little manipulation.

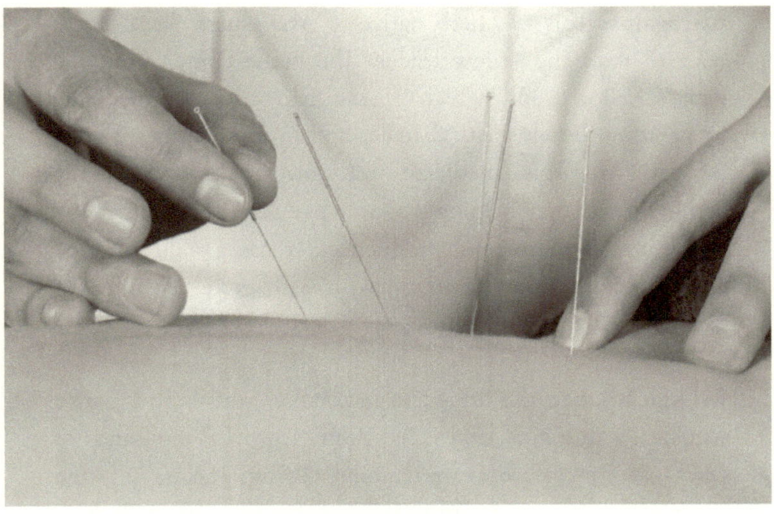

Chinese healers used two aspects of healing, much like traditional African healers: The passive (yin) and the active (active) - Yin and Yang. That provided a holistic approach to medicine and healing. Herbs were not necessarily ingested but also used within acupuncture in practices like moxibustion. Also known as moxa treatment, the healer would place small hot cones of the herb they were using like mugwort on top of the skin.

The cone will begin to burn until it reaches the flesh, and the skin starts to turn red. The healer will extinguish it, but it will have stimulated the flow of the patient's Qi (pronounced as "chee"). The Qi is instrumental in facilitating the patient's healing because it boosts the immune system and strengthens the blood circulation.

Typical Chinese herbal medicine worked by mixing several herbs rather than using an individual herb on its own. TCM (Traditional Chinese Medicine) focuses on issues like allergies, arthritis, diabetes, depression, joint pain, skin conditions, fertility, and obesity, among other ailments.

Some of the herbs used by ancient Chinese healers include:

Astragalus: This is a herb native to Asia where the Chinese refer to it as the yellow leader. The name comes from the plant's yellow root, which is the part used in medicine preparation. It helps with diarrhea and to combat night sweats in patients. This medicine was instrumental in many communities in helping boost patients' immunity by increasing immune cells' production. It has a mild antiviral effect, so sometimes healers mixed it with more potent herbs to make cold medicine.

Ginkgo Biloba: Also known as maidenhair, this herb is native specifically to China, and it has been grown for thousands of years. It is the only remaining living species of the Ginkgophyta order of plants. The leaves of the plant help with respiratory illnesses and to boost blood circulation.

The nuts were ground and used to make cough and cold medicine, reduce fever, and combat diarrhea. In some Asian cultures, they were a side dish. The extract from the leaves was a pain reliever.

Chinese healers favored the use of Ginkgo over other herbs because the plant is neutral. That means that it doesn't affect the body's balance, so it leaves the Yin and Yang intact.

Ginseng: China ginseng featured prominently in healing herbs used by Chinese healers. It was useful in reducing inflammation and also improving the immunity of the patient. Some healers gave it to men with erectile dysfunction and also used it to increase their energy levels. Ginseng seems to have aphrodisiac properties, and it also improves sperm count and quality in healthy men. It increases nitric oxide, which helps combat erectile dysfunction.

Gotu Kola: This is known as the herb of longevity used in TCM and Ayurvedic medicine. It is beneficial in healing skin conditions as well as helping in reducing swelling in bruised areas. Healers gave it to patients who were experiencing insomnia. Female healers gave it to women to help eliminate stretch marks.

Yu Xing Cao: This herb is also known as shepherd's purse. It belongs to the mustard plant family and helped treat menstrual disorders and blood circulatory issues. The shepherd's purse was helpful when people had blood in their stool or urine or even vomiting blood.

> "All that man needs for health and healing has
> been provided by God in nature, the
> challenge of science is to find it."
>
> — PARACELSUS

CHAPTER FOUR: THE HEALTH BENEFITS ASSOCIATED WITH HERBS AND SPICES

Good health is an integral part of life, and, like a desirable woman, you have to earn her through work and commitment. The good news is that nature provided for us through herbs and spices; all we need is commitment. Herbs and spices are associated with health and vitality in cultures and civilizations we have looked at previously. That is not a coincidence. The healing properties of spices apply to all the continents of the earth.

In India, it was in Ayurvedic medicine; in China, it was in TCM, in the Americas, and Africa; it was with their shamans and Sangomas. In Europe, it was in their apothecaries. But herbs were not only used for healing purposes. Here is a breakdown of herbs and spices identified by modern science according to their health benefits.

HERBS AND SPICES FOR LONGEVITY:

Anything that can grant life, and life eternal or increase it by a day is precious to humans. Our search for a longer life continues today, and we are willing to fake it till we make it. You must have come across all the anti-aging products and their relatives. Herbs and spices have shown incredible efficiency in increasing human life's longevity. In this case, we will look at survival in terms of life expectancy.

Herbs

Aromatic herbs have antioxidants that are incredible protectors against cardiovascular disease. Scientists believe that antioxidants prevent oxidative stress that damages organ cells like heart and kidney cell tissue. The antioxidants prevent changes that turn cholesterol in the blood into LPL, low-density lipoprotein, which accumulates and clogs heart artery walls. The plaque on the walls makes you susceptible to heart disease. Oxidative stress continues to increase as we age.

At the top of the aromatic herbs list packed with antioxidants, we have coriander, thyme, and sage. These herbs are rich in phenolic acids, carsonic acid, and rosmarinic acids that help circulate lipids that cause oxidative stress.

Sage

Sage is perhaps the queen of all antioxidant herbs. This herb has a notable amount of vitamins and rosmarinic acid that help prevent oxidative stress. Its antioxidants help to fortify your body's immune system so that other diseases will not invade your system. Drinking a cup of sage tea will lower your bad cholesterol LDL and increase the good cholesterol HDL. This herb also contains more than 160 polyphenols, which offer powerful antioxidant functions in your body. That results in a lowered risk of cancer and improved brain function.

The leaves of sage apply to the treatment of diabetes. These leaves have a grayish-green color and are edible, but you can use them in food or beverages. Sage is useful in diabetes treatment because it has anti-hyperglycemic effects on type 2 diabetic patients.

According to research by the Medical News Today Knowledge Center, sage also helps treat Alzheimer's disease. That is because the plant can guard against neurodegenerative diseases and enhance cognitive skills. In young people, sage can improve memory.

Nutritionally, it will help you lessen the need for salt, which can be highly unhealthy and addictive. It works well in meat dishes. When using sage with all the spices and herbs, it is advisable to work with natural forms like whole fresh leaves or dried, and ground leaves.

. . .

Coriander

Did you know that coriander is related to carrots and celery? Coriander has a sweet aroma, and you can use the seed or the leaves. For a little clarity here: cilantro and coriander are parts of the same plant. However, in the United States, cilantro refers to the plant's leaves and coriander to the seeds. In other parts of the world, they are coriander leaves or seeds.

Coriander features in the medical world for its ability to lower blood sugar levels. So people with diabetes who are on medication and other people with low blood sugar levels, like fasting people, are advised not to use a lot of coriander. The herb lowers your blood sugar by activating glucose inhibiting enzymes in your body. The proteins make the entry of the sugar into your cells difficult.

The primary antioxidants in coriander include tocopherols and terpinene. These offer neuroprotective as well as immune-boosting properties. Most brain ailments, including Parkinson's and Alzheimer's, are strongly linked to inflammation. This herb has active anti-inflammation properties, which help to safeguard your brain against these diseases.

It has some applications in helping patients with Alzheimer's disease improve their memories and cognitive skills. It also helps reduce anxiety nearly as effectively as when one is using prescribed medication like Diazepam.

Coriander's aroma makes it easy to consume in food and beverages. It adds flavor to all types of international cuisines and is useful in combating conditions like indigestion and Irritable Bowel Syndrome. It also decreases bloating, abdominal pain eliminating the discomfort that comes with these conditions. The herb also contains dodecenal, a compound that can help fight stomach infections like Salmonella.

If you have someone struggling with their appetite for various reasons like chronic illnesses, try some coriander. Coriander may help with boosting their appetite.

• • •

Thyme

Thyme is a close cousin to mint, but it has over 400 subspecies. It has a distinctive herbal taste with flowery undertones similar to rosemary and lavender. However, you can still pick up the minty flavor from afar and a hint of sweetness. It has remarkable antibacterial properties, which is why it is an effective natural cough medication. Drink some thyme tea next time you have a cough and feel the difference within hours.

In terms of longevity, this herb is an excellent immunity booster since it is full of Vitamins C and A. These vitamins help your body to build up defenses that prevent diseases from attacking you. Apart from boosting your immunity, this herb can help to manage whooping cough and bronchitis.

It helps stem the increased production of phlegm while reducing the inflammation of the upper respiratory tract. Thyme also has antispasmodic properties enabling it to prevent muscle spasms that cause coughing.

People with arthritis also found relief when they took thyme tea because it reduces inflammation in the joints. The thymol found in thyme is useful in dental settings where it is used in combination with chlorhexidine to make dental varnish. This combination will prevent tooth decay.

Mint

Mint is a general name for plants belonging to the Mentha genus. These include spearmint and peppermint, and they have a distinct minty flavor. The cooling effect of mint makes it a popular flavor in food, beverages, baked goods, and confectionaries. You can use mint in its fresh or dried form.

Mint is commonly used to combat Irritable Bowel Syndrome. It soothes your digestive system while also relieving the bloating and discomfort that accompanies the condition. However, it is essential to note that the mint is more helpful when used in oil form than in leaf form.

But don't rule out the mint leaves, which are super helpful in combating colds and coughs. You may notice that even over-the-counter medication cough and cold medication features a strong minty flavor. Mint not only cools the respiratory tract it also helps with the decongestion of the nasal passages, significantly improving your airflow and breathing.

Crushing the leaves to release the flavor is recommended rather than eating the leaves in your food. Crush the mint leaves and steep them in your beverages for a refreshing cooling drink.

Oregano

Oregano brings a strong, pungent flavor to dishes with just a slight bitterness and sweetness. But that is not surprising because, like thyme, oregano is also a member of the mint family. It is available as fresh leaves or in dried form. Oregano is full of antioxidants combating the harmful free radicals that make you susceptible to chronic diseases like cancer.

Oregano has exceptionally high concentrations of thymol and carvacrol, which are potent antioxidants. The two components also help fight off viral infections. It also contains potent antibacterial properties that help to grow certain diseases causing bacteria like Escherichia coli.

Some researchers found that using oregano extract on a human colon with cancer cells prevented the cells' growth and killed them off as well. These test tube studies have given the medical fraternity hope that oregano, with more research, can help patients fight cancer cells in the colon. The anti-inflammatory nature of oregano also helps to combat inflammation in your body.

Interestingly, you may notice that the leaves on an oregano plant have different flavors. Some leaves are distinctly mintier compared to others that have a traditional oregano flavor.

· · ·

Rosemary

Rosemary may have tiny leaves that could fool you, but don't judge a book by its cover. Those small leaves are quite fragrant, making the distinct smell of the plant ooze out of it. You can pop a whole sprig of rosemary into your food or beverage and release the herbs' flavor. Rosemary is also a member of the mint family of plants.

The herb has been used for a long time to boost the immune system and alleviate muscle pain. You can also use rosemary to improve your memory as it has anti-inflammatory properties. The leaves are useful in cooking and beverages. Chopping it up also releases the flavor, so you can throw it in the blender with other vegetables and make a green smoothie.

Rosemary helps combat indigestion, and the German Commission E has approved its use. The German Commission E. is the body that investigates and examines the efficacy and safety of herbs. The herb also prevents cancerous cells from growing and replicating in colon and breast cancer.

SPICES

Ginseng

This spice is proven to have potent antioxidants that help fight free radicals. The herb is excellent at fighting off inflammation and also increases the antioxidant capacity of your cells. That helps your cells grow strong and healthy. As a result, your immunity improves, and you can fight off disease and infections better.

Ginseng reduces oxidative stress by increasing your antioxidant enzyme activities. That is particularly important for people dealing with erectile dysfunction because blood vessels may be the problem. Antioxidation in your cells allows the blood vessels to move more blood, restoring normal function to your reproductive organs. Ginseng also improves the production of nitric oxide, which helps with the relaxation of muscles. As a result, there is better blood circulation to the penis.

The spice also helps recovering stomach cancer patients, improving their immune system. They also showed fewer occurrences of recurring symptoms. Patients who took ginseng also boosted their chances of living disease-free for longer after curative surgery.

Cinnamon

Cinnamon reduces the risk of heart disease and improves insulin sensitivity. It comes with heaps of antioxidant properties, including very potent polyphenols. It also has strong anti-inflammatory properties enabling your body to fight off infections and repair tissue damage. Chronic inflammation is usually against your internal organ tissue cells.

Using cinnamon in your food and beverages is an easy way to ingest the spice. Consuming cinnamon is not difficult because the spice is the epitome of deliciousness, and it can fit in all types of dishes, pastries, and hot or cold beverages.

Cinnamon also helps to cut the levels of harmful cholesterol molecules in your blood. It also stabilizes your good cholesterol and regulates your blood pressure keeping your heart healthy. The spice is also able to control your body's absorption of insulin. Most people's bodies are resistant to insulin absorption, leaving them vulnerable to high sugar levels. As a result, they are more susceptible to type 2 diabetes and metabolic syndrome.

Cinnamon will help you bring your blood sugar levels down. It does so by slowing down the breakdown of carbohydrates when it inhibits your digestive enzymes. Studies have found that cinnamon has a distinct anti-diabetic effect on blood glucose.

Paprika

Paprika aids in the healthy digestion of food, so it helps

prevent issues like indigestion. This spice comes from dried peppers of the Capsicum annuum plant. It has a distinct red/orange and yellow color that gives it a luxurious reddish look to the dish. Paprika is rich in antioxidants, minerals, and vitamins that promote healthy vision. From vitamin E to beta carotene, this spice also helps prevent macular degeneration because of age.

There are varieties of paprika with capsaicin, which helps prevent inflammation by binding to your nerve cells. As an inflammatory agent, it can also combat the pain and discomfort of arthritis and nerve damage.

Cholesterol (HDL) effectively lowering the risk of heart disease. Other components like lutein and zeaxanthin help fight off cancer cell growth and reduce oxidative stress. Capsanthin, another compound in paprika, is useful in raising good cholesterol.

HERBS AND SPICES ASSOCIATED WITH STRENGTH, ENDURANCE, AND SEXUAL PERFORMANCE

Ginger

Did you know that ginger increases blood flow enabling you to get more blood flow to your reproductive organs if you have erectile dysfunction? Many cultures consider ginger an aphrodisiac, and it even comes up in the infamous Indian book on sex and love, the Kamasutra.

The spicy yet sweet-smelling herb also invigorates you with its warm aroma, and the scent is not too overwhelming.

Garlic

Garlic is anything but sweet-smelling, but it is a powerhouse to boost sexual function. You may not want to consume garlic because you believe it to be a mood buster. But it is a booster to your blood flow, which means you have a stronger erection and enhanced sexual participation. Garlic contains high levels of allicin that facilitate more blood flow.

Also, garlic is excellent for your heart, and you want it strong to give you stamina and endurance during sex. It is important to note that some people like Sadhguru, the yogi mystic, believe that while garlic is potent medicine, they do not consume it every day. They believe that since it is medicinal, too much of it could negatively affect overdosing on any herbal medication like cannabis and ayahuasca. With this in mind, it may be ideal to use garlic on specific days in the week and not daily.

Cloves

Cloves provide the warmth in your body that enhances the blood flow into your muscles. Blood temperature and blood flow are crucial in getting your muscles pumping and active. According to a study in the Journal of Medicinal Food, cloves are excellent for infusing energy into your system. They also increase your stamina. All you have to do is place some clove into your teacup, and you may instantly feel energetic again.

Cloves contain eugenol, which helps to stabilize your sugar levels. When you feel tired and lethargic, it is usually because your blood sugar levels have dipped. By stabilizing the glucose levels in your body, cloves help you to recover your energy and strength. This spice also enables you to increase your testosterone level, which is crucial in both genders' sex drives.

Saffron

Saffron is an expensive spice, but a little goes a long way, literally. Not only can large quantities cause an overdose, but they will also cost you more money. The little you take will help you improve the blood flow and through the blood vessels. That enhances the sexual function of men, and it also increases the natural lubrication for the woman. Some women take saffron to help reduce the pain of their menstrual cycle.

Saffron is also a mood booster, and it invigorates you leaving you feeling more energetic. You can take it as an aphrodisiac when you do not feel like you are in the mood.

Cardamom

Cardamom is present in most Middle Eastern and Indian cuisines because it enhances the dish's flavor. It is also great for blood flow throughout your body. Cardamom contains cineole that improves blood flow into both female and male sexual organs.

The flavor has vitality, and it promotes well being while infusing energy into your body. These cultures use cardamom to beat fatigue and detox so that their energy levels do not dip.

HERBS AND SPICES RELATED TO THE HEART, BLOOD, AND LUNGS, LIVER

When it comes to spices and herbs related to the heart, blood, and liver, we will look at detoxifying plants that ensure your body is healthy.

Tarragon

Many people use tarragon to promote a healthy heart. It contains potent anti-inflammation properties that combat the chronic flare-ups that cause the heart to weaken. It is an excellent companion to meat dishes and all types of soups.

Tarragon is rich in manganese, which helps immensely with preventing oxidative stress. It also contains potassium that is crucial for healthy heart function because it lowers blood pressure. High blood pressure places stress on the heart muscles, making you susceptible to cardiac arrest.

. . .

Basil

Basil is a potent anti-inflammatory agent that can help fight off the inflammation that causes cardiovascular, lung, and liver diseases. Several basil species exist, including sweet basil, curly basil, lemon basil, Thai basil, holy basil, or lettuce-leaf basil. They all contain similar components that make them excellent for your heart, lung, and liver health.

For example, basil contains viceninaire and orientin, potent antioxidants that fight off all types of inflammation-causing free radicals.

Basil is also incredible at helping to clean the blood because it contains potassium. The potassium helps your kidney with fluid elimination allowing you to urinate more often, effectively removing toxins from your body. Try and have a combination of sage and basil in your tea after your meal.

Also, basil can help prevent fat from building up in your liver, ensuring that it is healthy and working at optimum.

Bay leaves

Bay leaves are also packed with potassium, making them an ideal herb for detoxification. That cleans your blood and helps your kidneys eliminate the toxins through water elimination. Also, because they enhance the taste of food, you don't need to add more salt. Salt increases the risk of cardiovascular disease and stroke.

Dill

Dill is full of vitamin C, a potent antioxidant. It has also been studied and found to normalize liver lipid accumulation. High accumulation of lipids in the blood vessels can lead to non-alcohol related fatty liver damage. The same fats can cause damage to your heart.

Dill significantly increases the presence of HDL, the good cholesterol in your blood. That will help combat the effects of bad cholesterol and improve your liver and cardiac health. Also, the healthier the liver, the more it regulates the metabolism of cholesterol.

Ginger

Gingerol in ginger is the main medicinal component that has potent antioxidants and anti-inflammatory properties. It can drastically reduce the risk of heart disease while also significantly reducing your blood sugar levels. It also lowers cholesterol levels allowing your liver to have a healthy amount of cholesterol to metabolize adequately. With the reduction in cholesterol markers in the body, you are less at risk of heart disease or liver damage.

Cumin

Cumin contains phenols that function as potent antioxidants. These antioxidants fight the free radicals that cause inflammation resulting in chronic diseases. Having antioxidants in your body means you can stabilize the free radicals and keep off the oxidative stress.

Patients taking cumin with their yogurt for one and a half months began experiencing increased good cholesterol HDL levels. The spices also lowered the bad cholesterol in the blood.

HERBS AND SPICES RELATED TO SKIN HEALTH

The skin is the largest organ of a human being. And perhaps the biggest benefactor of what herbs and spices can do. For example, chamomile can soothe and heal beard burn, while turmeric makes the skin glow.

Chamomile

Chamomile smells excellent, and the flowers hold the secret to the plant's soothing and healing properties. The flowers contain alpha-bisabolol, which helps diminish the fine age lines around the mouth and the eyes. The same component also helps heal skin irritations, including eczema and acne. You can also use it to treat minor burns.

Chamomile is easy to use as you can either drink it in your tea or steep the flowers in warm water and use it as a face wash. Alternatively, apply a chamomile tea bag on your face and leave it on for 10 minutes, then rinse your face.

Red clover

The red clover is easy on the skin, helping to soothe red, chafed skin or the itchy patches that come with eczema. You can use red clover topically or ingest it. The herb works by eliminating the toxins in your bloodstream that cause inflammations to flare up.

Drink tea infused with red clover by steeping some flowers in hot tea for half an hour. You need at least two to three cups a day to feel the effect. You can also soak the flowers in hot water, let it cool, and then use it as a facial wash.

Horsetail

This herb has a very high concentration of silica, which is a crucial element in skin collagen. It strengthens the collagen that, in turn, enhances the skin giving you excellent skin elasticity and hydration. The body produces collagen for the skin, which becomes depleted as you age. The less collagen your body makes, the more dry skin you get, and the higher the chances of getting wrinkles.

Horsetail tea is useful as a toner for your skin to soothe skin. Steep a handful of horsetail in 3 cups of hot water for at least fifteen minutes or even a couple of hours and use the resulting cooled down water for your face.

Rosemary

Rosemary has antiseptic properties, so you can use it to wash your face and disinfect it. That will leave you with a healthy, clean visage that will absorb other facial treatments better. Rosemary can also help get rid of spots and blemishes to give you a bright skin complexion.

The plant's astringent aspect enables the skin pores to tighten, making it look younger and refreshed.

Cinnamon

Cinnamon features powerful antifungal and antibacterial properties so it can combat acne. It is also a powerhouse of antioxidants that help with blood circulation to the skin giving it a healthy glow. When applied as a face mask, its astringent properties dry excess oils allowing healing to occur.

You can also apply cinnamon on eczema inflamed skin because it soothes the skin's irritation that leads to inflammation.

Green tea

Green tea is full of powerful antioxidants because it contains a very high concentration of catechins. The catechins give green tea its strong anti-aging ability and also act as anti-inflammatory agents. Because of this, you can use the spice on all types of skins. The topical application of green tea can also help to speed the healing process of your skin. That is in addition to evening out the skin tone and fading out spots. It inhibits an enzyme produced by your skin that causes you to have uneven skin pigmentation.

You can use it as a sunscreen to reduce sunburn and DNA damage to your skin. Apply some on top of your regular sunscreen for the best results.

Paprika

Paprika is among the family of hot peppers (cayenne, jalapenos, and chili) that can defend your skin. It contains loads of vitamins C and A that provide antioxidants to fight the free radicals. Free radicals cause premature aging—they breakdown your collagen causing your skin cells to lose their strength.

The pepper also contains capsaicin, which protects your skin from UV ray damage. Paprika and the other peppers work well only when you eat them because when applied topically, they will burn the skin.

Turmeric

All you have to do is turn on a beauty magazine or follow a beauty influencer, and you will find numerous ways of using turmeric for healthy skin. Turmeric contains curcumin, a potent antioxidant and anti-inflammatory agent. It helps to heal the skin by reducing oxidation and improving the work of collagen.

According to the National Psoriasis Foundation, it also enables you to control inflammation flare-ups in conditions like Psoriasis. The foundation advises using it in your food to harness its benefits and enjoy the flavor at the same time.

You can also use it as a face mask to prevent acne scarring. It is an effective way to eliminate the scarring that comes with acne breakouts. It is also an excellent treatment for scabies. Scabies leaves a rash on your skin because of microscopic mites.

HERBS AND SPICES RELATED TO STOMACH AILMENTS

Peppermint

Peppermint is easy on the stomach because it is a potent antispasmodic agent. A stomach ache or cramping can be a result of gastrointestinal muscles experiencing spasms. By easing the cramps, peppermint lessens the discomfort of stomach pain. It also soothes Irritable Bowel Syndrome by reducing the stomach's inflammation that results in gas and bloatedness.

Fennel

Fennel seeds help you to relax the gastrointestinal system, which helps reduce stomach cramps. As a result, you have less gas, and it also acts as a diuretic allowing you to pass more urine and free your system. Fennel also contains a lot of fiber to help you have a natural bowel movement.

Parsley

Parsley is excellent for indigestion, whether you eat the parsley leaves or drink tea made from the parsley plant seeds. It can also work wonderfully on heartburn easing the painful sensation. That is because it acts as a diuretic and also gets rid of gas. Also, the alkaline nature of herbs, like parsley, neutralizes the acid reflux in the stomach.

Chamomile

Chamomile flowers steeped in your tea is helpful for cramps and stomach upsets. Women having menstrual cramps will find a cup soothes them to sleep and eases the pain. It works by preventing the muscle spasms that cause menstrual cramping.

• • •

Ginger

This spice is a superstar spice as it features almost everywhere on helpful herbs for the human body. Ginger can wake up a sluggish digestive system. A slow digestive system can contribute to indigestion as food is not moving at a healthy pace. Ginger also stimulates saliva and also increases the production of bile. It is also quite effective at helping you get rid of gas.

Cardamom

This spice is excellent at balancing the environment in the stomach. It balances the mucus, bloating, and gas in both your stomach and small intestine. It goes well in cooked dishes, but if you come across cardamom in your chai latte, don't pass it up, especially if your stomach is agitated. It will soothe it right away.

HERBS AND SPICES RELATED TO BRAIN FUNCTION

Black pepper

The piperine in black pepper improves your brain's function by inhibiting the enzyme that breaks down serotonin. Serotonin relays messages from one part of the brain to another and influences your body's psychological processes.

It influences the brain cells that control your mood, sleep, and social behavior. An imbalance in serotonin can affect your behavior, like the mood and social mannerisms making you depressed.

Black pepper also effectively works to lower depression symptoms like anxiety and lethargy. Adding black pepper to your food or beverage can add a little pep in your step. The spice also forestalls the aging process for the brain, helping to prevent conditions like Alzheimer's.

According to the 2006 "Journal of the American Geriatric Society," black pepper improved the ability to recover in stroke patients. Some patients inhaled an infusion of black pepper oil for one minute, which activated their brain's region that controls your swallowing reflex.

Saffron

Saffron has a high concentration of carotenoids, which increases healthy levels of serotonin. The increased levels of serotonin ensure that you experience feelings of happiness. Ingesting saffron also helps you to reduce mild to moderate feelings of depression.

According to studies done on using saffron on patients with mild to moderate Alzheimer's, the conclusion was that the spice works effectively, at least in the short term, to improve the patient's cognitive function.

Cinnamon

Cinnamon can help you become more alert and improve your cognitive function, even if it is only the scent aspect. Smelling cinnamon can help improve several memory tasks that you may associate with the spice. For example, in baking or cooking, you can remember cinnamon recipes easier than recipes with no lingering scent.

The spice reduces inflammation levels, and inflammation causes brain disorders like multiple sclerosis, Huntington's disease, Parkinson's disease, Alzheimer's, and stroke. The presence of antioxidants in the cinnamon helps to mitigate the inflammation with the utmost effectiveness.

Turmeric

The curcumin in turmeric is the primary antioxidant ingredient that helps reduce inflammation. With the inflammation taken care of, your brain can remain healthier and more alert for longer. You can quickly sprinkle it on food or drink several times a day to boost your brain function.

Ginkgo Biloba

Ginkgo biloba is useful in improving concentration and memory. It also prevents oxidative stress and protects your brain through the process of aging. You can use it in its dried herbal form or as a liquid.

Lemon balm

Lemon balm is incredibly excellent for the nervous system. It is a very calm herb, and it also boosts your mood. Using lemon balm also helps improve your cognitive speed. You can concentrate better on whatever you are doing and use it in multiple ways.

You can create tinctures, cordials, infusions, and herbal syrups. You can also take it as a capsule or in the form of a fresh herb.

Bacopa

In Ayurvedic medicine, this herb holds a place of esteem as a neuroprotective plant. It is a bitter herb, but it is also very energizing. In Ayurveda, it is considered a rejuvenating herb that gives you vitality and keeps your brain alert.

You can use the herb if you are having trouble concentrating, and it will help you with retaining information, focusing on a task, and soothing your senses to reduce mental fatigue. Some students have taken it to help them with alertness in their learning processes and improve their mental clarity. You can take it as a tincture, capsule, or dried herb.

Bacopa is also know as water hyssop. It can also repair damaged neurons and improve neuron communication. It also protects the brain cells from chemicals that can cause cognition and memory-related diseases.

And God said, "Behold I have given you every herb bearing seed which is upon the face of all the earth and every tree in which is the fruit of a tree yielding seed: to you it shall be for meat."

— THE HOLY BIBLE (GENESIS 1:29)

CHAPTER FIVE: COMMON AILMENTS AND HOW HERBS AND SPICES ARE TIED TO TREATMENTS AND PREVENTION

Alternative medicine is not always the first option because it is unregulated. Also, clinical evidence in terms of efficacy can be lacking due to a lack of adequately documented clinical trials. Herbs and spices have been there for centuries, and there is no denying their treatment and healing potential. There is plenty of accumulated anecdotal experience in the Orient, cultures that are more appreciative and sensitive to herbs and spices' power than the west.

More accurate methods of studying herbs and spices help bring to the fore their power, influence, and potential applications that can help treat ailments such as stroke.

The World Health Organization (WHO) is recognizing herbs and spices. The organization defines traditional medicine as, and we quote:

> *"Practices, approaches, knowledge, and beliefs incorporating plant, animal and mineral-based medicines, spiritual therapies, manual techniques, and exercises, applied singularly or in combination to treat, diagnose and prevent illnesses or maintain well-being."*

This definition is crucial because it helps dispel the notion that traditional medicine is to displace pharmacology. It complements and works in combination with modern medicine for better outcomes. In some applicable cases where proven, it can serve as a singular alternative approach for maintaining well-being.

Here are some common ailments and the role of herbs in their treatment:

Stroke

For the most part, most people know that a stroke has to do with the interruption of blood flow to vital parts of the brain. But to be more precise, a stroke occurs when there is a reduction or discontinuation in blood supply to parts of your brain. As a result, there is not enough oxygen and nutrients to the brain tissue. The brain cells begin to die in minutes. A stroke demands speedy medical attention to mitigate the damage done and the physical challenges that may ensue beyond suffering a stroke.

While any person can suffer from a stroke, the most predisposed groups are over 55 years of age. Men are at a higher risk of suffering a stroke than women. However, women too suffer strokes but at a more advanced age, and the results are less likely to be fatal than men. It's also worth noting that hormone therapies, pills, and contraceptives involving estrogen increase the risk level of suffering a stroke. Treatments for stroke are dependent on what type of stroke one has suffered. In ischemic stroke, the treatments work to break up clots and restore blood flow to the brain and prevent further brain cells from dying.

According to the 2018 guidelines from the American Heart Association (AHA) and the American Stroke Association (ASA), it mentions that treatment is most effective when administered within 4.5 hours from the commencement of a stroke. When applied early enough, this treatment can minimize brain damage. Other therapies give attention to reducing complications and preventing additional strokes.

In the case of hemorrhagic stroke bleeding in the brain, treatment will depend on the location, cause, and extent of the bleeding. Surgery may be necessary to alleviate swelling, intracranial pressure, and prevent bleeding. Certain medications such as painkillers, diuretics, or corticosteroids can reduce swelling, and anticonvulsants to control seizures.

HERBS THAT HELP TREAT A STROKE

Asian ginseng - Part of Poststroke therapy building and stimulating memory in a patient. Asian ginseng, also known as Panax Ginseng, appears to boost brain chemical acetylcholine activities. It is a substance in the brain that's involved in memory. Ginseng is an ancient herb that has worked as an effective treatment for various neurological disorders for the past 2000 years. Today, ginseng is beneficial for helping with recovery from a stroke and other acute and chronic neurodegenerative diseases. Ginseng is neuroprotective.

Researchers today acknowledge that ginseng and other traditional herbs and spices warrant a more in-depth look and study. The role of ginseng and its saponins in stroke prevention and treatment has sparked a lot of interest in the medical fraternity. A closer look at ginseng has revealed various mechanisms in which the herb contributes to the treatment of ischemic stroke.

Astragalus - Astragalus membranaceus is a traditional Chinese herb. As we know, many patients who suffer a stroke make only a partial or inadequate recovery. About 36% of acute hemorrhagic stroke patients at discharge will remain moderately to severely disabled. With such high morbidity and mortality associated with this condition, alternative treatments to enhance the patient's recovery are necessary.

Pharmacological studies have demonstrated that herbs such as astragalus are helpful. They possess antioxidant, anti-inflammatory, and anti glutamate properties. Such herbs can be useful post-treatment of stroke because of their ability to dilate blood vessels, suppress platelet aggregation, protect against ischemic reperfusion injury, and enhance the tolerance of ischemic tissue to hypoxia.

Astragalus membranaceus is widely used in China as a drug to facilitate recovery after a stroke. Clinical studies performed in China indicate that the herb does enhance stroke patients' recovery from their neurological disability to improved functional outcomes.

HEART DISEASE

Many people have lost loved ones to cardiovascular disease. A sobering and staggering statistic is that one in four deaths in the United States is related to heart disease. The term "heart disease" can be used interchangeably with the phrase "cardiovascular disease." Cardiovascular disease is a general reference to conditions involving narrowed or blocked blood vessels that can then lead to heart attacks, strokes, and chest pain.

Heart disease is not as simple as it sounds. You are mistaken to believe it is only one condition. Much like thyme that has many subspecies, heart disease can mean any of several conditions under the same umbrella. These include but are not limited to coronary artery disease or heart rhythm problems, known as arrhythmias, and congenital heart defects. These are heart problems that one is born with. Another condition is dilated cardiomyopathy. They occur when the heart cannot pump blood properly due to dilated heart chambers due to heart muscle weakness. There is also myocardial infarction, known as heart attack or coronary thrombosis. It occurs because of the development of a blood clot in the coronary arteries or sudden narrowing of an artery.

Leading a healthy lifestyle that incorporates eating nutrition that is low in cholesterol, exercising regularly, and getting enough sleep can go a long way in keeping fit. A healthy lifestyle can help you overcome obesity and manage sugar levels well enough to reduce heart-related diseases.

Spices and herbs are great for seasoning our food. But some everyday condiments that we may take for granted are perfect for heart health. They have natural properties with the capability of reducing inflammation. Inflammation is a significant driver for arterial disease development and plaque ruptures that can lead to heart attacks.

HERBS AND SPICES THAT HELP TREAT HEART DISEASE

Cinnamon - Given that 70% of heart attacks are a direct result of insulin resistance. It is quite promising to learn that consuming a spice such as cinnamon in the food improves people's insulin sensitivity without diabetes. That directly translates to fewer chances of suffering a heart attack with regular intake of such spices in tandem with leading a generally healthy lifestyle. This spice is delicious food and significantly reduces blood sugar, triglycerides, and LDL (bad) cholesterol while improving good (HDL) cholesterol for overall better heart health.

Turmeric - Consumption of turmeric has immense benefits. That is because the spice naturally contains a potent anti-inflammatory and an antimicrobial compound known as Curcumin. This compound is beneficial in killing oral bacteria and can help patients suffering from periodontal gum disease. Why is this important? 50% of people aged 30 and above in America are likely to suffer from gum disease, which happens to be one of the leading contributing factors that cause arterial disease.

Garlic - Garlic has long been prescribed as a heart tonic by physicians for more than 2000 years. Garlic is known to lower blood pressure and boost heart health. Consuming a clove or half a clove of garlic every day reduces cholesterol levels by 9%. Also, taking aged garlic can bring down systolic blood pressure by 5.5%. By regularly consuming this aromatic plant in your food, you can help drastically reduce the chances of suffering from cardiovascular disease.

CANCER

Cancer is an abnormal growth of cells. There are more than 100 types of cancer. We commonly know breast cancer, skin cancer, colon cancer, lung cancer, prostate cancer, and lymphoma. Symptoms of cancer patients will vary depending on the type of cancer that one has. The cancer treatment may include radiation, chemotherapy, and surgery.

While medicines and medical procedures have their place, physicians encourage healthy eating that includes herbs and spices, which can help prevent abnormal cell growth or what we know as cancer. Some herbs with naturally occurring compounds such as phytochemicals are known to stimulate the body's immune system and potentially help keep the dreaded disease at bay.

Turmeric - This spice is not only tasty in food but has impressive health benefits. Turmeric is useful in spicing up soups, stews, and sauces. It is an excellent chicken rub or seasoning for veggies. The active ingredient in turmeric is the compound curcumin. Curcumin can undermine these blood vessels and choke and strangle cancer cells to death.

Saffron - Saffron is one of the most expensive spices you can encounter, as mentioned earlier. However, it's well worth its weight in gold because it packs a good punch in several ways. It is tasty and contains the compound crocins, a water-soluble carotenoid that inhibits tumor growth and cancer progression.

Oregano - Among herbs and spices, oregano features the most abundant source of antioxidants. This herb also has potent antibacterial properties and is a natural disinfectant. It is known to slow cancer growth by promoting cell death, also called apoptosis.

Cayenne Pepper - For those who love their food hot with pepper, this hot pepper will flavor your food while also providing a compound known as capsaicin, a powerful antioxidant. The spice contains anti-inflammatory qualities in addition to beta-carotene. Beta-carotene is known to be toxic to cancer cells and helps prevent the growth of cancer cells.

ALZHEIMER'S DISEASE

Alzheimer's disease is a progressive disorder that causes brain cells to degenerate and die. It is the leading cause of dementia, which eventually deprives patients of the ability to function independently. It does this by causing a continuous decline in social, behavioral, and thinking skills.

More than 5 million Americans of all ages have Alzheimer's. Statistics show that by 2050, that number will have skyrocketed somewhere to the tune of 14 million. Symptoms of Alzheimer's in the early stages include being forgetful of conversations and recent events. Eventually, patients with this disease will develop severe memory impairment and lose their ability to accomplish everyday tasks. Presently, the condition has no cure. Medication is to try and slow the rate of decline and maximize function for as long as possible.

Can herbs and spices be of any benefit with Alzheimer's

disease? Herbs and spices may very well be the key to suppressing inflammatory pathways by acting as antioxidants and inhibiting acetylcholinesterase and amyloid-beta aggregation.

Ginko leaf - The Ginkgo tree has been around for the longest time and is arguably considered one of the world's oldest tree species. Because of ginkgo's ability to increase circulation and is laden with antioxidants, it is of little wonder that many alternative medicine specialists advocate its use in helping with the early stages of Alzheimer's. It can even help prevent the onset of dementia and its symptoms like short term memory loss.

Turmeric - Turmeric extracts whose active ingredient is Curcumin help block beta-amyloid formation, responsible for the plaques that hinder brain function in Alzheimer's disease. India's population, which consumes more turmeric, has far fewer numbers of Alzheimer's diseases than the States. Is it a coincidence, or does the disparity in turmeric consumption levels between the two nations have something to do with turmeric's power?

Ginseng - A contemporary look at the herb by Korean researchers at the Kyung Hee University reveals that black ginseng protects against ischemia-induced neuronal and cognitive impairment. It is also beneficial in helping vascular dementia.

DIABETES

There are three main types of diabetes. These are Type 1, Type 2, and gestational diabetes. The most common form of diabetes is type 2, and about 90 percent of people with diabetes suffer from it. This type of diabetes begins when cells fail to respond to insulin appropriately. We might all be better off by focusing more on herbs and spices in our diets to help prevent diabetes.

Cinnamon - Cinnamon contains bioactive components that can help lower blood sugar levels and affect fasting plasma glucose, LDL cholesterol, HDL cholesterol, and triglyceride levels in patients with Type 2 diabetes. A sprinkle of 1 to 2 grams of cinnamon in tea, smoothie, or oatmeal can help keep diabetes at bay.

Fenugreek - Due to Fenugreek's seed hypoglycemic activity, they can improve glucose tolerance and lower blood sugar levels. That is in addition to the provision of fiber content that slows down the absorption of carbohydrates and sugars.

Ginger - Ginger is a root herb with numerous benefits. The hypolipidemic and anti-oxidative properties of ginger are beneficial in regulating blood sugar levels. Ginger is also known to improve insulin sensitivity, reduce oxidation, and improve cholesterol levels, which is all good for the prevention and management of diabetes.

OBESITY

Being obese or overweight places an individual in a high-risk category for diabetes and heart disease conditions. But with a regular exercise routine and healthy nutrition that includes herbs and spices, one can reduce their susceptibility to the mentioned health conditions.

Fenugreek - Fenugreek seeds help with appetite control and effectively reduce food intake to support weight loss for obese persons.

Cayenne pepper - The active medicinal ingredient in cayenne pepper is capsaicin. It reduces appetite and hunger to promote weight loss.

Oregano - Oregano contains carvacrol supplements, directly impacting some specific genes and proteins that control fat synthesis in the body. That helps with fat metabolism.

ANXIETY AND ANXIETY DISORDERS

We all get anxious from time to time, before a big interview, as we await results, and during life-changing moments. Those feelings of tension and worry are part of our lives. However, fear and the stress, and all other associated emotions can become a norm due to their frequency of occurrence. When the situation gets there, it is no longer only anxiety; it is an anxiety disorder. It could be one of the following:

Generalized Anxiety Disorder - Also known as GAD, chronic anxiety occurs even when there is nothing to cause fear. One experiences exaggerated tension and worry.

Panic disorder - Panic disorder is unexpected bouts of anxiety accompanied by physical symptoms. The symptoms include chest pain, shortness of breath, heart palpitations, nausea, dizzy spell, and stomach upset. Panic disorder can be debilitating, especially if the bouts are consistently repetitive.

Obsessive-Compulsive Disorder (OCD) - It is a condition where one has an obsession with certain things or sequences of events. It comprises repetitive behaviors known as compulsions. These become rituals that you, when not performed, resulting in uncontrollable anxiety.

Social Anxiety Disorder - Also known as social phobia, it is characterized by excessive self-consciousness in social settings. It can be manifested in fear of public speaking, being around members of the opposite gender, or even eating in public places. In its most severe form, it can occur in almost all settings where one is around strangers. In mild ways, it surmountable as soon as one gets comfortable in their new environment.

Post Traumatic Stress Disorder - PTSD is anxiety that develops after one experiences a traumatic or terrifying event in their life. It can develop after a natural disaster, as a victim of violence, or after surviving an accident with fatalities. It can also be because of military combat experience.

Anxiety, in whichever form, needs to be taken with

seriousness. No one likes the feeling of being anxious, whether for a while or for a long time. Here are some useful herbs that can help patients with anxiety navigate through life with more calm.

Chamomile - Chamomile leads the pack because it has a calming effect on the senses and the nervous system. It soothes you because it has phenolics, including quinones, flavonoids, and phenolic acids.

Lavender - The relaxing floral scent of lavender flowers are incredibly relaxing and is used liberally in aromatherapy to calm down the senses. You can make a lovely cup of lavender tea at home and drink it to soothe yourself after a long day. In centers where they study brain activity, lavender has been used as a relaxant and sedative to help patients sleep better.

Brahmi - Brahmi has a definite effect on anxiety because it increases the serotonin levels in your brain, countering anxious thoughts. It also sedates the brain without dulling the senses. Instead, you have sharp focus and clarity.

Ashwagandha - This herb reduces cortisol levels, also known as the stress hormone in the body. Cortisol levels shoot up when one is stressed, increasing your anxiety levels, and it also contributes to more in-depth issues like depression and chronic insomnia. Ashwagandha helps one to feel mentally calm even in stressful situations and is a good relaxant.

SOME HERBS AND SPICES CAN CAUSE AILMENTS: THINGS TO WATCH OUT FOR

Traditional herbs and spices have been used correctly as additives to foods. Some herbs such as ginger and cinnamon go very well with beverages or food. Since they also come in a capsule supplement form, it is best to consult with your physician before consuming any. That is to be safe and overrule any foreseeable health issues such as allergies. Also, it ensures that you take the supplement in the right dosage.

The problem comes in when you overuse the herbs. They say too much of anything is poisonous, and that includes herbs and spices. However, the good news is that most herbs do not have extreme side effects. For example, using too much turmeric will cause you to experience a bit of a stomach upset or diarrhea. Some people may feel nauseous as well when they take too much turmeric, especially in their beverages.

Ginger can cause heartburn when used excessively. Some people have reported that it can cause throat irritation. It also has caused dermatitis in people with susceptible skin. Garlic is used cautiously because of the spicy scent one's breath acquires after ingesting it. Fennel may cause your blood clotting to slow down. The herb also has a component that works like estrogen, so if you have hormone-sensitive conditions, it is best to steer clear of fennel.

It would be best to take basil in recommended doses because it acts like fennel by limiting your blood clotting abilities. Saffron causes dry mouth, sweating, and nausea when taken in high quantities. You may also experience a change in your appetite, and some people develop an allergic reaction to it.

Bay leaves may cause you to be tired and sleepy. That is because bay leaves work as a sedative in traditional herbal medicine.

Lastly, pepper can be delicious and also very hot. It may cause you to have diarrhea, and if you suffer from anal fissures, they can exacerbate the pain and discomfort. Anal fissures are small tears in the anus, and when they come in contact with the heat from the pepper, you will experience a burning sensation.

*"A society that keeps cures secret so that they can
continue to sell medication for high profit is not
a real society but a huge mental institution."*

— DR. SEBI

CHAPTER SIX: GROW OR BUY

If we were to be completely honest with each other, we would raise the fact that some of us belong to the microwave generation, which only pops things into it for a minute or so, and voila, it is ready. We are not particularly fond of working hard, and neither do we have the time. When presented with growing, which involves actual work and buying, which spends our money, we are happy to purchase. We prefer the ease and convenience of purchasing.

But some of us prefer to grow our plants, especially in this world of overuse of fertilizers and pesticides. Besides, producing not only gives the assurance of quality but also ensures availability when needed. Growing versus buying your herbs is a raging debate, with environmentalists vouching for the former. The choice depends on the individual.

If you choose to buy your herbs and spices, you have to be extremely vigilant about specific things to ensure that you get the best herbs possible.

WHAT TO CONSIDER WHEN BUYING HERBS AND SPICES

Age

Unfortunately, spices and herbs can stay on the shelves (both at the supermarket and home) for too long and lose their health benefits. The average shelf life of spices and herbs is six months. After this, the nutrients in them can be affected by light, and they become less and less potent and effective.

Irradiation

The irradiation process utilizes radiation to give the spices longer shelf life and prevent pests from destroying them. The good news is that irradiation doesn't make the food radioactive. However, according to some consumer organizations like the Organic Consumers Association, the process causes the spices to lose nutrients.

It also damages the food by creating free radicals that adhere to chemicals like pesticides to create URPs (unique radiolytic products). They also claim that science has not yet proved that long-term consumption of a diet of irradiated foods is safe for humans.

The alternative is to buy non-irradiated spices, which may mean you have to source your herbs from local farmers who offer home packed spices. These tend to be fresher and still in their natural form. You can also buy from health food stores.

Buy whole

To ensure you are buying fresh herbs, buy them whole and grind or dry them at home. For example, purchase entire sprigs of rosemary rather than dried and packed options. You can also buy whole peppercorns and grind them as you need.

When buying the spices and herbs, use your nose. Smell

them to ascertain how fresh they are—the more potent the smell, the fresher the batch. If you don't smell the spice, it has probably been on the shelf for too long and has lost its potency.

Don't buy bulk

However, if you are going to opt for fresher herbs and spices, it is good to buy smaller quantities that you can use extensively and finish sooner. That eliminates the problem of keeping your spices on the shelf for too long. You will get the most out of your herbs and use little with excellent results.

Also, make sure that you store them in optimum conditions to serve you for a long time after buying your herbs and spices. A cool, dry, and dark shelf is ideal, and the spices and herbs do well in an airtight glass.

Avoid gourmet spice shopping

Some gourmet shops will sell you common spices but at an inflated price. They will use their products to entice you, but you can access the same herbs at lower prices at ethnic markets near you.

There is an important question that people ask: "Why take a chance on stale, irradiated spices when I can grow my own?" That is a great idea! But before you embark on this delicious journey, you need to learn a little bit about herbs. You can do this by visiting your local gardening store or nursery. You will be able to buy your seeds from her, but you also learn how to care for the plants to get you started.

THINGS YOU NEED TO KNOW ABOUT GROWING
YOUR HERBS

Plant cycles

Among the things you need to learn is whether your herbs

are annual or perennial plants. Annual plants have one life cycle. Every year you have to grow a new plant. Plants like basil and coriander are examples of annual plants.

Perennial plants can keep growing season after season, so you don't have to keep planting new ones every year. They will continually bloom year in year out. Perennial plants are best grown as seedlings, while annual plants are best as seeds. Thyme and mint are perennial plants.

Watering plants

Your herbs need water to grow because the moisture helps the plant move the nutrients from the roots to other parts like the leaves, flowers, and fruits. The water is absorbed by the roots, which are in the ground around the plants.

However, make sure that you do not overwater the ground. Too much water will wilt the herbs, and it makes them lose their flavor.

Fertilizer

Fertilizer helps your herbs to have the best nutrients, including nitrogen, potassium, and phosphorus. You can opt for commercial or organic fertilizer because each provides the plant with these nutrients. Nitrogen helps the plant make leaves; potassium helps fight off disease and strengthens the plant, while phosphorus makes strong roots.

It would help if you found the right balance for watering and fertilizer application so that the herbs thrive.

Sunshine

Your herbs need plenty of sunshine to grow healthy. Most of the herbs that we enjoy are native to the hot Mediterranean climate. That means that they thrive with lots of sunlight. The sun's heat helps them develop essential oils that infuse the plant with its great flavor.

The light from the sun makes the plant's food through the process of photosynthesis. A herb receiving plenty of light will be robust with plenty of flowers, leaves, berries, and fruit that you can harvest. However, also make sure that the sun is not too hot to burn the herbs. Consider applying mulch on the herb to prevent moisture loss if the temperatures are too high.

Soil

Make sure you choose healthy, fertile soil for your herbs. If your land is poorly cared for, it will yield a very poor harvest. Unhealthy soil limits the absorption of carbon dioxide for photosynthesis and also blocks out sunlight.

Harvest

You need to continually pick your herbs often to keep the plant producing a new crop regularly. The pruning will encourage growth in the plant. Even if you harvest a lot more than you need, you can always freeze the fresh herbs in airtight containers.

Space

Don't place the plants too close together because each herb needs plenty of room for the leaves and roots to branch out. At the garden store, you can ask about the spacing requirements for the herb you are buying.

Growing Your Herbs

You can grow your herbs in your garden, in a pot or in a community garden.

. . .

In a pot

Potted plants are not just practical, but they can also offer your space a beautiful aesthetic. They look great, whether you have them indoors or outdoors. Herbal plants are extremely rewarding container crops. But like all plants, your herbs can get out of hand if you let them grow unattended.

When planting your herbs in a pot, you can control the plants' size by limiting the container's size. However, some herbs do better in deeper pots because their roots need to extend far or wide down into the soil. Herbs that are grown in containers need moderate watering to control the amount of water the plant receives.

Select pots that feature suitable drainage holes. That ensures that the excess water that is not absorbed by the plant drains out. As a result, they are not swimming in the water and losing their flavor in the process. Your pots should all be at least 6 inches in diameter to allow adequate room for growth. It is okay to get larger containers for herbs that tend to spread like mint. The best container herbs include mint, Coriander, Parsley, Sage, Chives, Thyme, Rosemary, Bay, and Basil.

Once you buy the potted seedlings, you have to re-pot them into larger pots that allow them the room to grow. Make sure the new pots are at least twice the size of the seedling pot. Place your containers in a spot that gets plenty of sun.

PROS OF POTTED PLANTS

Clean the air

Placing potted plants indoors helps to infuse fresh air into the environment as the plants use carbon dioxide for photosynthesis and produce oxygen as a result. However, you may need to put out the plants during the night because they revert to using oxygen and releasing carbon dioxide without the sunlight.

Increases humidity

During transpiration, the herbs release excess moisture into the air. That increases the humidity in your space, making the air easier to breathe in, especially in the dry, hot months. In the colder months, you can keep the plants outdoors.

Portable

You can carry potted plants and place them anywhere you want. That allows you the flexibility to have the plants in your house and outside according to your convenience.

CONS OF POTTED PLANTS

Missed sunlight

Depending on where you have placed them, they can miss the sunlight resulting in a poor harvest. You have to keep moving the pots where the sunlight is if you are working with an enclosed space.

Pots dry faster

Pots tend to dry out more quickly because of the drainage holes, especially during the hot and windy months. Because of this, you may need to water your herbs twice a day.

More nutritional needs

Potted plants have limited soil, so their roots can't extend further to find additional nutrients that they may need. That means you have to give them more fertilizer to make up for the deficiency they may experience as they grow.

Buy soil and containers

It is crucial to buy soil for the plant, unlike gardens where the earth naturally occurs there. You may have considered getting earth from your yard, but experts recommend getting dirt that has met specific growth requirements for your plant to thrive. You have to buy the containers for aesthetic purposes, especially if the pots will be indoors.

In the garden

Herbs thrive in the garden, and the good news is that your garden doesn't have to be huge to give you a good yield. Your yard is a good enough patch for you to start your herb garden. But planting in a garden is much more involved than growing in a pot.

To begin with, you need to prepare the soil. Clay heavy soils need to have some compost added to infuse them with helpful organisms and essential nutrients. Incorporating compost is a recommended step for pretty much all types of soils. However, it is advisable not to use too much compost manure because as much as they give the plants a growth boost, they can also reduce the flavor.

Garden grown herbs have access to the rain. However, in soils where there is questionable drainage, like sandy and clay soils, it is best to make raised beds for the herbs. That means that your herbs grow in more fertile soil contained in the beds off the ground. You may need to buy the earth for the raised bed. Ultimately, raised gardens offer the perfect conditions for your herbs.

When it comes to watering, make sure that the herbs get a maximum of 2 inches of water weekly. That entails leaving the soil dry to the touch on some days; then, you can resume watering. If you have herbs that need slightly more moisture, consider mulching to prevent too much water loss and keep the soil adequately wet.

Harvest garden herbs regularly to encourage even more

growth. You can provide fresh herbs for your friends and family if you have too much supply. Harvesting the herbs is more of a trim than a hack. Cut off the tips but don't trim the plant closer to the bottom.

The best garden herbs include Rosemary, Dill, Arugula, Marjoram, Thyme, Tarragon, Sage, Lemon verbena, and Oregano. You should group the herbs that need more moisture together and the dry ones separately. This way, your watering approach is simple, and you can tend to each plant as it needs.

PROS OF GARDEN-GROWN HERBS

Bountiful harvests:

Most herbs are generous if you give them attention and care, plus they are not too demanding. Even with a little space in your garden, you can get a bountiful harvest. All you need is the right arrangement. The perennials even keep producing as you harvest, so you don't run out. That is an excellent environment for people who love to cook or use herbs because it ensures that you always have herbs available at any moment. You can cook whatever you want to at a moment's notice and all because of your effort. Nothing beats the feeling of pride and achievement from seeing a harvest from your work.

Saves money

Most people think that gardening is hard work; well, it can be. However, most herbs are easy to grow, and except for the initial cost of setting up, they mainly require water and some love. Since you have more variety in a herbal garden, you don't have to buy any of the herbs you need to cook. As a result, you have more money in your pocket, and you spend less time shopping for herbs that may be unavailable at your local grocery.

• • •

Curb appeal

Having a beautiful green garden makes your yard look beautiful and exciting. We all want to wake up to greenery and beauty. Herbs like chamomile and lavender feature flowers that make the space gorgeous. And the scent! Excellent, filling scent of life, health, and healing.

A fun hobby

Having a garden is a fun hobby for most people, and it helps your ecosystem thrive. You provide herbs for yourself and your family and food and home from the little animals in the nearby ecosystem. Gardening can be a stress beater for you. The best part is that you can include your family, friends, and even neighbors, bond, and have a great time together.

CONS OF A HERBAL GARDEN

Space

You must have some land to be able to grow your garden. If you do not have a yard, you may have to "borrow" some land from the community land.

Time-consuming

Tending a garden is more time-consuming compared to managing a potted plant. You have to buy more fertilizer and spend more time watching the garden to get the results you want. The truth is, it is an investment that needs your physical presence to thrive.

In the community gardens

A community garden is a shared public space where a collective group of people plants different things. It is an excellent option for city dwellers who want to have a place to source their fresh herbs in their neighborhood.

Raised beds will work exceptionally well with community gardens because they do not alter the land's original layout. If land reclamation occurs for any reason, the gardeners do not lose their herbs. Instead, they can move their gardens elsewhere without interfering with their hard work.

You can go the traditional route of planting an in-ground garden on the plot of land. But if you are using raised beds, you should expect a bit more work. You need some wood to make the beds where you will be planting your seeds. The bed features side borders but no bottom. It is out in the sun, and you can put some fertilizer in the soil.

Make sure that the ground is level to allow the bed to sit correctly. The bottom of the bed should feature broken up earth to enable the water to drain and accommodate the roots of the herbs you grow. Fill the beds with soil and compost, as well as some minimal manure. That ensures that the earth is nutrient-rich. The soil in the bed is prone to dry out quickly, just like with a potted plant. So with raised beds, you will have frequent watering.

The best herbs for a community garden may include Basil, Mint, Chamomile, Lavender, Coriander, Bay leaves, Parsley, Dill, Chives, and Rosemary. Feel free to experiment with as many as possible; you have everything to gain.

PROS OF COMMUNITY GARDENS

Beautification

Community gardens are great spaces that beautify the locale where you find them. Most vacant lots look horrible because they have no one maintaining them. With the community garden in place, the space looks vibrant and has a lot of attention.

Sharing

People share their herbs and their time as they participate in activities like watering the garden or mulching and preparing the planting spot. It is an excellent place to show solidarity with neighbors and teach young ones about caring for their environment.

Access to fresh herbs

Everyone in the community has access to fresh herbs. This garden adds value to all the members of the community. Fresh produce can be hard to come by, especially in urban neighborhoods.

However, you have your source right in your community, giving you healthy food at all times.

CONS OF COMMUNITY GARDENS

Different opinions

It can be hard to work with such a large group of people in harmony. One has to practice a lot of patience. You also have to follow the leadership that you may find in place. There may be some clashes, but most of these are quickly resolvable with no hard feelings.

Waiting

As much as vacant lots may be present in your locale, they may not be available for use, or you may have to get on a waiting list to get approved for a community garden. Be patient and wait while following up with the authorities.

Vandalism

Vandalism can occur in community gardens if not adequately secured. Sometimes members can steal from each other's patches if the garden is in small individual plots. You may also lose expensive gardening tools to each other and even outsiders. Of course, regulating harvesting from the garden is paramount. Everyone must follow strict rules to keep the project sustainable.

. . .

Keep pests and insects away

The smallest pest can be your biggest problem. We are talking about aphids, snails, and slugs. But since herbs are plants that we ingest, it is recommended to avoid chemicals and commercial pesticide to combat this problem. Instead, try some of the home remedies at your disposal.

Interestingly, some of the herbs you are planting can be repellent to insects and other pests like rodents. Peppermint is an excellent example of such a plant. The scent of mint repels aphids and other insects like ants. Although many people shy away from planting mint because it is a very aggressive grower, you can opt to plant it in a pot and cut sprigs, and lay them in your in-ground or raised bed garden to repel pests. The scent of mint repels even rats. Other herbs that are natural repellents of insects and pests include lemongrass, fennel, basil, and catnip. You can also treat your garden with everyday substances like salt and flour.

As you grow your garden, it is good to learn how to make organic DIY pesticides instead of relying on commercial insecticides. Here are some recipes to help you get started:

Soap spray insecticide: Mild soap can act as a very effective insecticide when added to a quart of water. It will kill off aphids, beetles, whiteflies, and other mites. Spray the mixture on your herbal garden in the morning and evenings when the temperatures have cooled down for the best results.

Oil insecticide: This is a simple recipe that includes vegetable oil and mild soap. Put a tablespoon of the soap in a cup of vegetable oil. Shake thoroughly and store. When you need to use it, place a quart of water and two tablespoons of the mixture in a spray bottle, and use it liberally in your garden.

The oil coats the pests, effectively depriving them of air and eventually suffocating them.

Neem oil pesticide: Neem is a natural herb that has strong insect repellent properties. Using this insecticide will halt the natural life cycle of pests and eradicate them from your garden. The oil produced by the neem plant is not toxic to human beings or animals, and it is also biodegradable.

Garlic insecticide: The pungent scent of garlic comes in handy in deterring pests and insects from invading your garden. This insecticide will not necessarily kill off the insects, but it will prevent them from entering your garden in the first place. You can use it together with some homemade chile pepper spray.

Make an intense garlic spray using two whole bulbs of garlic (not just two cloves). Blend them until they completely dissolve in your blender. Add one quart of water into the resulting puree and leave overnight. In the morning, strain the mixture and extract the garlic-scented water. You can add some vegetable oil or some mild soap to help the liquid stick better to the plants. If you are using it with Chile pepper, you can also add the peppers to the garlic during pureeing.

Tomato leaves insecticide: Did you know that tomato leaves can help with repelling insects? Just chop the leaves of the tomato plant, which contain alkaloids known as tomatine. Steep the chopped leaves in water and leave for a couple of hours, even overnight. Strain the liquid and spray liberally in your garden. It will control aphids, mites, and other insect pests.

"One day is not enough to green our earth. Planting caring and love is also expecting our earth from us. Do it, it will heal not only the land but also your body and soul."

— KARTHIKEYAN V

CHAPTER SEVEN: STORAGE AND CONTAINERS

*S*ince herbs and spices are available in everyday cooking, it is prudent to buy an amount that you can use for a couple of weeks without running to the market in search of more. If you are planting them in your garden, you want to harvest enough and give the plant enough time to generate a new batch for you.

Most spice and herb vendors will tell you that their products don't spoil. There is some truth to this. This book has already established that they often lose their flavor, aroma, and even color. In some cases, the turmeric is not as flavorful or striking reddish-yellow as it should be. The star anise doesn't have the same strong licorice scent, and the cinnamon is lackluster.

But to be fair, you may buy the freshest, most aromatic, and flavor-packed spices and herbs, but you don't store them as you should. When you buy your herbs, you will probably see on the label a shelf life of 1-3 years. However, these are irradiated products. You can use non-irradiated spices for 10-12 months with excellent storage. But it is advisable to use them within six months of purchase.

HOW TO STORE YOUR SPICES

Storing your species is unlike nailing jelly to a tree and hence, should not give you sleepless nights. You have plenty of options available for you allowing you to keep spices and herbs in different containers. We will discuss some of them.

Glass - Glass is a favorite container material because it can keep air out. Air is a significant factor that affects the quality of the spices and herbs over time. Spices that cake do so because they came into contact with air, which has moisture. Glass is not porous, so there is no way air can ever find itself into the container once it is closed and secured. You can ensure this by using glass containers with cork tops. These containers are also great because you can see the state and quantity of your spices.

However, when you use a glass container, you have to be extra careful because it can break easily. Also, glass containers easily let light in, altering the state of some spices and herbs.

Plastic - You can use plastic containers, which are a cheaper alternative to glass. However, plastic comes with challenges like being porous, allowing in some airs and odors that affect the herbs and spices' quality over time. Also, plastic made from BPA can impart harmful chemical components into your spices.

Plastic is also commonly used for spices because most companies package their spices in plastic containers for retail. It is even easier to recycle plastic containers at home and use them to store your spices and dried herbs.

Metal - Metal is another popular option because it is cheaper, and it is completely non-porous. Also, metal is the most durable option of all the containers. When you choose the metal to use, it is best to work with rust-resistant options like stainless steel.

However, when using metal containers, it is crucial to ensure that the place you store them is away from heat. Metal is a conductor of heat, and this can impact the state of the spices and herbs.

Ceramic - Ceramic is an expensive but very efficient option. They protect your ingredients from all factors that will affect your herbs and spices, including air, humidity, and light. They are also the most aesthetically pleasing option. You can buy them at a bargain in vintage shops or at thrift shops.

Re-sealable paper - Pouches and paper bags are useful to store fresh herbs if you place them in the refrigerator. The reusable pouch's inner lining is usually lined with plastic or foil material to help with the storage of dry spices and herbs. Some options feature biodegradable lining.

WHERE TO STORE HERBS AND SPICES

Before deciding where to store your herbs and spices, you may want to know what affects all types of spices and herbs—having a good understanding of how factors such as humidity, air, heat, and light will help your growing process.

Air - Spices are hygroscopic, meaning that they attract water from the atmosphere. Air contains moisture, so spices naturally absorb the moisture, which, unfortunately, degrades them. The flavor is the first component of spices to be affected by the humidity. It also affects the weight of the spices and herbs, so you have to use more to get the preferred results.

Humidity - Some spices naturally produce water vapor increasing the humidity of the storage area. It is crucial to have containers that can keep out the moisture. For example, black pepper will introduce water vapor in the air affecting moisture-sensitive spices like cinnamon. It is best to store black pepper separately in a glass, metal, or ceramic container to prevent this. Humidity also promotes mold growth in your spices. Mold will introduce mycotoxins into the spices, so you may get foodborne ailments when you cook with them.

Light - It would help if you considered dark-colored glass containers to keep light out. That will prevent issues like oxidation of the spices, which will degrade their flavor. Ceramic vessels are excellent for keeping out the light.

Heat - When spices and herbs come into contact with heat, their oil dries out. The oil contains all the spice or herb's flavor, so destroying it kills the product's essence. Please do not keep spices in direct sunlight or near the stove close to the heat. Because of these factors, keeping your herbs in the dark and a cool place is always advisable. The ideal temperature for storing your spices is below 70 degrees Fahrenheit. Once you get the perfect temperature, keep it constant.

SIGNS OF SPICES AND HERBS THAT HAVE GONE BAD

The goodness of spices and herbs lies in their freshness. The fresher, the better. However, sometimes we buy a lot of them, or our cooking motivation goes down, meaning that we may find ourselves with a batch that has stayed for a while. While you can use your nose and put your sense of smell to test whether your spices are suitable for use, there are other ways of checking for the same. You can check for:

Mold - Mold is one of the main signs that your spices have gone bad. The moldy smell tells you that the spices have had proximity to humidity and moisture. There will probably be a fuzzy substance growing on the spice or herb.

Discoloration - If the spice has either lost its original color or has a different color, it is not safe. You can tell the difference because the spice or herb is not as rich in hue as it originally was.

Taste - If the spice muddies the food's taste instead of imparting the rich flavor and aroma, it is no longer safe to use. It would be best if you disposed of the entire dish to be on the safe side. If your spices begin to taste bitter where they should be sweet, it is time to throw them out.

"Like people, plants respond to extra attention."

— H. PETER LOEWER

CHAPTER EIGHT: TEAS, WATER WITH ADDITIVES AND OTHER DRINKS

Some of us associate spices with food only, and true; they bring out the best in food. The burst of flavor with each bite is almost magical and keeps us hooked to good food. However, it doesn't only have to be food. Beverages are another leading way to consume these products of nature. Drinks infused with these plants have taken inspiration from age-old traditional healing practices.

As we become more health-conscious and move towards drinking healthy green juices, herbs and spices make these drinks tastier. It is not fun to drink down a glass of kale and spinach, no matter how good it is for you. However, a little cinnamon flavor in there can make it more palatable.

When it comes to alcoholic beverages, you may have tasted some spicy varieties like a basil mojito garnished with candied jalapenos. Sounds delicious and lethal at the same time. How about a paprika salt in a chili mojito? These spices and herbs make the drink fun while at the same time, packing it with flavor.

HISTORY OF SPICING ALCOHOLIC DRINKS

From the Far East to Europe and Africa, the annals of history hold alcohol consumption and brewing stories. In ancient Greek literature, entire passages were cautioning against excessive alcohol consumption. The population favored mead, an alcoholic beverage made from water and honey that was fermented. Sumerians were early beer makers, and they had over 20 recipes.

. . .

Wine

The Greeks and Romans spiced their wine, which was known as mulled wine. Mulled wine originated in Rome, where the citizens would heat their wine to warm their bodies over the cold months.

Mulled wine is heated wine with spices and herbs like cloves, ginger, cinnamon, and honey to sweeten it. They used fruity red wine to create mulled wine, and this remains the most popular type of wine to spice to date. With time, the concept of mulled wine spread worldwide as far as Sweden as the Roman Empire expanded.

Today mulled wine has become a global phenomenon, and countries continue to create their blends. You will find mulled wine on Christmas tables alongside mulled cider. Mulled cider is just as ancient as mulled wine, but it is a British drink made from cider, nutmeg, cinnamon, and orange slices. It could also contain peppercorns and star anise to give it a punch. It was drunk during the festive season, which coincided with the coldest months of the year.

Beer

Before introducing hops in the brewing of beer, making beer tastier was by adding spices and herbs. In fact, in many specialty beers, especially of the Belgian variety, this remains the norm. The popular herbs used to spice beer included juniper, anise, coriander, fennel, and dill.

These were chosen and are still in use today because they have a bitter taste, just like hops. However, they add a delightful flavor to the drink, making it even more compatible with different flavored dishes.

Beers were also flavored using spices like cardamom, clove, cinnamon, licorice, and nutmeg. New age beer brewers experiment with flavors like vanilla, pumpkin pie, orange zest, and saffron.

Allspices, cardamom, and cinnamon were common in medieval medicinal beers, while anise and caraway were famous for making beer bitter. Beers used in festivals had uplifting flavors from spices like cinnamon, clove, nutmeg, mace, and pepper.

Rum

Rum came from the Caribbean among sugarcane plantation slaves who discovered molasses could ferment into alcohol. Molasses is a by-product of the sugar refining process.

Spiced rum is a commercial venture introduced by the brand Captain Morgan in 1984. They spiced their brandy with caramel and spices like Star Anise, fresh ginger, and vanilla bean. Following spiced rum, other types of hard liquors like whiskey also began to offer spiced varieties.

It is important to note that this variety of spiced drinks doesn't have a medicinal aspect like the mulled wine and medicinal beers of old.

HISTORY OF SPICED NON-ALCOHOLIC BEVERAGES

The Chinese culture led the pack when it came to civilizations that consumed spiced non-alcoholic beverages. They were followed closely by the Middle Eastern cultures. These cultures used spices in the teas to add more flavor or as a medicinal beverage.

Flavors like cardamom and cloves were popular in the Arabic culture, and they were common right after having a meal. They were also available in the early evening with fruits like dates. In China, Laos, and Tibet, tea blended with spices came in small cups for medicinal purposes. It was for nourishment all day long, and they use larger mugs or glass jars as it became a beverage.

The Arabian culture made tea by cooking the herbs or spices in hot water, but the Chinese would place the spices in the cup and pour water onto them, and steep them as they drink it. They would use the same herbs all day long and add hot water to brew a fresh cup each time.

In Chinese culture, tea drinking increased human wisdom and took the spirit into a higher orbit. The legendary Chinese Emperor Shennong brought the original idea of tea drinking. Interestingly, the discovery of tea was by accident. The emperor had a rule of boiling drinking water. During a trip, his court was resting and boiling drinking water. Nearby leaves dropped into the boiling water infusing it with a brown color. The emperor was intrigued by the leaves and wanted to taste the water.

He drank some and found it to be refreshing. That was the beginning of drinking tea, and for a long time, this was the only definition of tea. It was and remains the national drink of China. However, the Chinese came up with different tea varieties, including oolong tea, green tea, yellow tea, and Pu'er, all of which are traditional tea derivatives.

Green tea - Green tea comes from the new shoots of the tea plant. The new sprouts dry before processing. The tea has a distinct green color, and it tastes distinctly herbal.

Pu'erh or pu'er - The is tea produced from a large leaf variety of tea bushes. The processing entails compressing the into a brick of tea leaves using a precise technology. Pu'er tea can either be ripe black tea or raw, green tea.

Black tea - Black tea is the second most popular type of tea consumed in China and globally. It is made from tea leaves that have been fermented and dried, resulting in a vibrant red hue. It has a subtle aroma.

Dark tea - Dark tea undergoes fermentation using bacteria. The process removes water and rolls the tea leaves several times before baking and drying.

Oolong tea - Also known as blue tea, this is unfermented tea created from a blend of red and green teas. The resulting tea is aromatic with a full-bodied flavor. It is favored for its distinct taste and even thought to help in breaking down fats.

White tea - It is a weak tea that slightly colors the waters. It comes from uncured and unfermented green tea, so it has a very subtle herbal flavor that is delicate.

Even though these teas don't have spices, you can opt to do so. However, connoisseurs of Chinese tea love the natural flavors of tea. Some people love to spice their tea with spices like lemongrass, ginger, and even onion.

HISTORY OF WATER INFUSED WITH SPICES

Infusing water with herbs is a relatively new phenomenon. You can buy water infused with herbs in grocery stores. But the good news is that it is easy to do in the home.

COLD WATER WITH HERBS AND SPICES

Cold water can feature herbs as long as you chop up the flavorings. Pour the water onto the spices and leave the water in the glass for a few minutes.

You can also lightly crush the herbs and pour water into them. Place the water into an ice cube tray and freeze them. You can use the water as you need.

HOT WATER WITH HERBS AND SPICES

Hot water can also feature herbs and spices. It is a simple process of steeping the herbs and spices in boiling water for a couple of hours. Remember, the Chinese continuously steep their tea and herbs in hot water to have a cup of tea all day.

You can drink hot water when you need to decongest your nasal passage infused with herbs and spices. You can also use the steam from the herb infused water to help with decongestion. This water also helps with your digestion and aids with constipation. Hot water infused with herbs and spices can also help improve your circulation and even decrease your stress levels. If you don't like to drink cold water, infuse some herbs into your hot water and drink slowly to get hydrated.

JUICES AND SMOOTHIES

You have to admit the best part of the juicing trends is creating delicious smoothies and juices from fresh veggies and fruits. Eating a mango is excellent, but juicing is even better, especially since you can infuse it with flavorful herbs and spices. A plain glass of mango juice pales in comparison to one infused with ginger or mint.

ADVANTAGES OF JUICES AND SMOOTHIES

Detoxification

Smoothies and juices are great for detox. When you consume juices or smoothies infused with fresh herbs and spices, you can help your body clean out harmful toxins. These toxins make it hard for you to absorb nutrients from your food optimally. Herbs like cilantro and turmeric are excellent for detoxification.

· · ·

Weight loss

Eating raw is a healthy way to manage your weight as you eliminate too much sodium and trans fats from your diet. Plant-based diets are also achieving massive popularity. Herb and spice-infused smoothies and juices are at the forefront of weight loss programs. The spices and herbs make the juices and smoothies taste better while at the same time giving your body their beneficial properties.

Nutrient absorption

Did you know that the majority of the nutrients found in fruit are within the juice? When you juice your fruits and vegetables, you can get a drink with more concentrated vitamins and minerals. The liquid form makes it easier for your body to absorb the nutrients. As a result, you have more intake of essential minerals and vitamins.

To benefit from the fruit or vegetable fiber, you can put some of the resulting pulp back into the smoothie. It will not only be beneficial for your gut health, but it will also be more satisfying.

Easier consumption

It is easier to consume juices and smoothies because of their liquid form. You can quickly drink the two on the go, like when driving or even when walking. That means you can make a larger batch of juice or smoothie and consume it at any time.

THE BEST HERBS FOR SMOOTHIES, SHAKES, AND JUICES

Rosemary

Rosemary has a piney scent that you can use in a juice or a smoothie. This herb is excellent for imparting minerals like calcium, iron, and vitamin B6. Drinking a smoothie or juice infused with rosemary will help with concentration and improve memory. It also helps with your digestion. Use some orange zest together with the rosemary to give the drink a zing.

Lavender

The lavender scent is calming, so you can make a juice or smoothie infused with this flower in the evening to help you relax. Lavender is rich in calcium, iron, and vitamin A, which help with strengthening of the bones, and also helps to ease bloating. You can take the infusion to de-stress your mind.

Basil

Basil is super refreshing with exotic flavors, including limonene, citral, citronella, and eugenol. Having some juice infused with basil gives you anti-inflammatory properties to fight off the free radicals that cause aging. It is very rich in calcium for healthy bones, vitamin C for great skin, and potassium to fight inflammation.

Tarragon

Tarragon infuses a fantastic herbal scent to a smoothie. It also adds antioxidants to your body. Antioxidants help with anti-aging. Because the aroma is heavy and herbal, it goes well with a strong flavor like orange or lemon.

Sage

Sage has a beautifully delicate flavor, and it is a powerhouse of vitamins A and K. The vitamins give it an antiseptic quality. The aroma is very calming and relaxing. Sage is also an astringent, meaning you can use it on your skin.

. . .

Dill

Dill has a sharp and tangy taste. It is delicious in sweet juice like orange or apple juice. That is because they infuse a bit of tartness that pricks your taste buds. You can also use it on a citrus blend of juices to add some more zestiness.

Dill is full of vitamin C and A. Vitamin C will help you with aging because it gives you a good dose of antioxidants. The additional vitamins are great for keeping your immune system at optimum. Chop up the dill and puree it, then strain it and get the extract. For smoothies, blend the dill into the drink, and you can even chew some bits of dill.

Mint

Mint is an exciting flavor that gives you a refreshing after taste and, of course, the cooling effect. This herb lowers your blood pressure and cholesterol levels in addition to being tasty. You can use the mint with peppercorn, and you will have an exciting kick. Mint is excellent for calming your senses and relaxing your anxiety.

> *"The gods created certain kinds of beings to replenish our bodies; they are trees and the plants and the seeds."*
>
> *— PLATO*

CHAPTER NINE: COOKING WITH HERBS AND SPICES

Since the discovery of spices and herbs, they have become part of many kitchens' pantries. For some people, they are a necessity, and food prepared without spices and condiments is bland. However, others prefer their food natural, while others do not know how to cook with herbs and spices. Whichever category you belong to, you are welcome to learn more about the use of spices and herbs to obtain the most benefits. Besides, cooking with herbs and spices can be a lot of fun. You are allowed to experiment with different spices and herbs, and with time, you will form your signature dishes to share with others. However, when you are cooking with these ingredients, there are some rules to follow.

RULES TO FOLLOW WHEN USING HERBS AND SPICES

Always check the expiry date

When you buy spices and herbs from the local grocery store, you always need to check the expiry date. Please don't purchase any products without an expiry date on them or a looming expiry date. If you are purchasing fresh products, make sure that you immediately store them in a secure container. Also, use them within three to six months if you have bought them in bulk.

Using expired spices and herbs can ruin the taste of your dish. Even if the spices haven't expired but have been on the shelf for long, they lose their flavor, forcing you to increase the measurement to achieve the taste you want. Keep in mind that as soon as you open spice, they begin the aging process. To make sure that you are using useful herbs and spices, mark the date you opened them to keep tabs on the passage of time.

Use sparingly

When using spices and herbs, the rule of thumb is always to remember that a little goes a long way. Take a pinch only to spice up your food if you are looking for a delicate fragrance. Go with half a teaspoonful when you want more aroma and flavor. Some spices and herbs are used in even smaller quantities so that the recipe will ask for only a dash. That is as little as 1/16 of the teaspoon.

As you add your spices and herbs, it is best to keep tasting the dish to ensure that you haven't overdone the flavors. When you find yourself with too much of a particular herb in your recipe, begin removing the leaves or sprigs to discontinue any additional flavoring.

However, if you have used chopped leaves of herbs like rosemary, basil, thyme, or bay leaves, you can dilute the dish by adding more ingredients and condiments. For example, if you make a pasta dish, adding more pasta can dilute the intense flavor and you can throw in some more tomatoes, onions, and coriander. That helps counter the overpowering taste of the rosemary or thyme.

If you are worried about making too much food, you can freeze half the dish for consumption later within the week. Alternatively, you can sweeten the food or make it more savory to distract from the overpowering herb or spice's intensity. Some people also make the dish more acidic by increasing tartness—foods like yogurt, sour cream, citrus, tomatoes, and vinegar work exceptionally well.

The best approach to using herbs and spices is crushing fresh herbs in your hand before using them in a dish. That applies to bay leaves, basil, oregano, and thyme. Alternatively, you can also chop them up. By doing so, you release the flavor from the leaves, and you end up using far less.

Additionally, you should measure your spices using a dry spoon to get the right amount. Sprinkling herbs or spices directly from the container into the pot on the stove is not a good idea. Not only does the rising steam find its way into the container, which ruins the potency of the remaining spice, but it also increases the possibility of more than you intended falling into the pot.

Lastly, you should not use spices and herbs to obscure the taste of your food. You will end up doing this if you use too many spices and herbs in the same dish. Remember that these products are for enhancing the natural flavor of your food. You still want to taste and smell the food.

Go fresh

Chefs advise using fresh herbs when you are cooking foods that require extended periods of simmering. That explains why specific meat cuts will be boiled or roasted with an entire sprig of rosemary, thyme, or whole bay leaves. The truth is that fresh herbs are not as potent as dried herbs, so you need to cook them longer to impart the flavor. But fresh herbs guarantee that you are using ingredients that are not past their expiration date.

Some fresh herbs keep their flavor and may even become more robust when they are frozen. Dill, oregano, basil, mints, lemon verbena, lemon balm, parsley, and rosemary are among them. Just wash them and pat dry, then chop them up. Please place them in a plastic bag and flatten them thoroughly to remove any air.

You can also puree fresh herbs and mix combinations with olive oil. For example, puree thyme and sage to make a paste and add some olive oil to them. Store this mixture in a freezer bag and use as needed. Just make sure you use it soon, within a couple of weeks.

Go dry

Dried herbs are three times more potent compared to fresh herbs. Whereas you may have used one tablespoon of fresh herbs in a dish, you will only need a teaspoon of the same herb in its dried form for the same recipe.

To get the most out of your herbs, you can buy them fresh and dry them yourself. The best process to dry your herbs is to air dry them. It is a slow process, but it retains the herbs' essential oils that contain the flavor.

To air-dry your spices, tie them up in small bunches using twine and hang them outside in direct sunlight, hanging upside down. A cord is great because as they dry up and shrink, it is easier to tighten the string. Once the herbs are dry, you can break them up and store them in the containers.

Another way to dry your herbs is by placing them in the oven. Spread out the leaves or seeds on a cookie sheet and place it in the oven at low heat. The best heat is below 180 degrees Fahrenheit. Let them toast for 2-4 hours. Unfortunately, this method results in the herbs losing their potency because they cook a little during the process.

Add at the end

Add herbs and spices near the end of the cooking process. That gives them the most flavor, but this works best if you use one herb or spice. If you are using multiple flavors, it may be best to add them at the beginning of the cooking process to blend them well.

It is important to note that pepper flavors increase in intensity as you cool them. As such, you may want to be very conservative with them in terms of measurement, and also, they should be the last addition to the dish.

Invest in relevant tools

Investing in a grinder is an excellent idea if you are embarking on this journey of using spices and herbs. Herbs and spices produce their flavors, even more, when they are ground. That means you can use them at the end of the cooking process to minimize the chances of cooking off their flavor.

Having a grinder is convenient, and it is easier to work with whole herbs and spices at home. This little device also ensures that the quality of your herbs and spices does not deteriorate. As long as they remain in their original form, herbs and spices do not undergo oxidation, degrading their quality. Using the grinder, you can grind the little that you need for the dish. It also gives you different options for grinding. The coarser the grind, the milder the flavor, and the finer grind will get more taste.

A grater also comes in handy when dealing with herbs and spices, especially in their whole form. Grating these ingredients into your dish is the ultimate way to enjoy the flavor of herbs and spices. Look for the smallest grater to ensure that you have a fine grate for a better flavor release.

You can also opt to remain traditional like your forefathers. The standard mortar and pestle is still an efficient way to get the flavor from your herbs and spices. Besides, it is age-proven to be a useful tool, non-sophisticated, readily available across the world, and most importantly, it gets the job done. There are also modern versions, including hand crushers.

• • •

Toast them

Some people like to toast their spices to release more flavor. It is possible to do this for both ground and whole spices but keep an eye on the heat to prevent burning the herbs. Toasting spices wakes them up, same as blooming them. Blooming spices is the process of cooking your spices in hot oil to release their flavor into the oil. The oil is for cooking your dish, imparting the flavor of the herb.

Learn winning combinations

Like humans, not all herbs and spices go well together. Some cannot stand each other; others merely tolerate each other, while others are best friends. Interestingly, others work together like salt and pepper. You need to understand each herb or spice's characteristics and pair it with a suitable partner. For example, if one is sweet, you can have another sour to create a balance. You do not want to have two strong and potent flavors together as they take your dish through a war of flavors, destroying it in the process. You can think of it as balancing a good team. If everyone is aggressive and dictatorial, then the team cannot function. Let us look at some combinations.

Sage and thyme are excellent companions, and rosemary goes well with tangy citrus flavors like dill. That is because one herb is sweet, and the other is tart. However, turmeric and cinnamon may not be a perfect combination because each is very potent and distinct. There will be a competition in which none will come out the winner. Instead, you will have a very confused dish.

Also, when using peppers, it is a good idea to understand the makeup of the pepper. Some are hot without much flavor, and others are full of flavor but little heat. Add the latter to already flavored dishes to increase the heat and the former to spicy food to impart more flavor. Cayenne is hot without too much flavor, and red peppers are flavorful, and some have a lot of heat as well.

. . .

Never double measures

If you have to scale a recipe up, do not automatically assume that you need to double the measure of spices or herbs. Begin with the usual standard measurement you use for the dish and add it according to the taste. If you automatically double the amount, you will probably over-saturate the recipe with too much flavor.

How to use herbs and spices in salads

Salads have a terrible reputation for being bland. However, with a little spice or herbal addition, they can go from being commonplace to becoming a tasty part of your meal.

There are five salads categories, including appetizer salad, accompaniment salad, main dish salad, fruit salad, and dessert salad. For better understanding, here are simple explanations of each.

Appetizer salad - The appetizer salad is a small portion of salad made of lightweight components that stimulate your appetite. It typically features small fruits like grapes and crisp, bright greens like lettuce. It comes at the beginning of the meal. Simple spices and herbs are all you need for this type of salad. The aim is to stimulate the taste buds, so keep it delicately flavored.

Black pepper: black pepper has a delicate scent and a mild zing that tingles your pallet, stimulating your saliva.

Lemon balm: This herb has a combination of mint and the bright taste of citrus. It opens the pallet while also stimulating the taste buds with the sweet flavor. It is also a great way to revive the taste of a limp tasting salad.

Pepper: A little heat can help stimulate your digestion and wake your taste buds up. Drop a tiny pinch of cayenne with lemon juice and some olive oil as a light dressing.

Accompaniment salad - It is the salad that comes with your entrée. It comes on a side plate and consists of light vegetables like lettuce tossed in a vinaigrette. The accompaniment salad should balance the main dish. That means that when you are eating a heavy main meal, keep the salad light. And when consuming a light main dish, go heavy on the salad.

In the accompaniment salad, you can use any of the herbs that complement the dish you are enjoying. If you have a meat dish with a hint of rosemary, you can incorporate some zesty herbs like lemon balm to complement the taste of rosemary. This salad can have very diversified flavors, and you can dress it up with spices in the dressing of choice. However, make sure that you go easy on the sauce.

Basil: You can use some basil in this salad even if you have it in the dish. The taste of basil in the salad will complement the cooked flavor. However, if you will use it in the salad, reduce the amount in the food.

Cilantro: Cilantro works well as an ingredient in an accompaniment salad for any dish. The aroma of coriander is refreshing and earthy, grounding the taste of any food. It is one of the herbs that can be a staple in all your accompaniment salads.

Mint: Mint is an excellent choice for an accompaniment salad because it refreshes the pallet, allowing you to enjoy the other main dish's different flavors. It can also complement certain natural flavors in meats like poultry and lamb.

Fennel seeds: salads with cucumber go very well with fennel seeds because the two flavors marry nicely. Going by this, it is a good idea to have fennel seeds accompanying a straightforward salad with almost bland ingredients like lettuce and cucumber.

Red chili: Chilli flakes can be incredibly flavorful in making salads. They add an exotic fruity flavor to the veggies.

Chives: Chives have a delicate onion flavor without packing on the full-on oniony taste. It is an incredible herb to add to any rice dish because the flavor beautifully complements the carbohydrate density.

However, hard herbs like thyme and rosemary should not feature in salads. The previously mentioned are just examples, but you can use any herbs because there are no hard rules in making your salad accompaniment salad.

Main dish salad - This salad is the actual main dish. Such salads feature a carbohydrate like pasta or rice, some form of protein like bean sprouts, or salmon bits and veggies. The main dish salad should be completely satisfying. Serve it in meal-sized portions, and it can be served hot.

Dandelion: If you like a little bitterness to your main salad dish, consider the dandelion. It infuses an adequate amount of bitterness to the overall salad dish making it more interesting. The tartness complements some of the cheeses used together with this type of salad, including feta.

Ginger: Grate some ginger and use it to spice the salad's meaty components like poultry or beef. Cut up slivers of the meat and incorporate it into the salad. You can also dress with a ginger-infused dressing. Ginger complements bitter herbs like dandelion and basil.

Garlic: Garlic has a spicy scent, but it works very well in the salad's cooked components like the macaroni and rice. Some people do not mind eating it raw as part of the dish. You can crush the garlic and mix it into the salad while it is still hot.

Turmeric: Cook the meat component like the chicken breast using turmeric. You can also sprinkle some more onto the salad to flavor it and enhance the turmeric's essence.

To make the herbs pop in the salad, cook the ingredients with dried herbs, and then use the same spices in their fresh form to garnish. For example, cook the pasta with dried basil and garnish with fresh basil leaves. There is a massive range of herbs and spices you can use to make main dish salads. Treat with your taste buds on this one.

Dessert salad - These are salads that come at the end of the meal, and they feature sweet ingredients. The dessert salad can have fruits, vegetables, whipped topping, mayonnaise, and candied components. The dessert salad goes very well with spices, especially those used on the candied parts. For example, if you are using candied jalapenos, you can add a cinnamon kick to make them even more flavorful. Herbs work in dessert salads, but spices can offer an alternative fun flavor at the end of the meal if you use them in the main dish.

Star anise: The licorice flavor is a fantastic accompaniment to jellos and other gelatinous ingredients of any dessert.

Fresh dill: This herb has a tart taste to contrast the sweetness and spiciness of components like candied jalapenos. You can sprinkle just a small pinch onto the whipped topping to give it flavor as well.

Borage: This is a beautiful, flowery herb that can garnish your dessert, and you can eat it simultaneously. You can eat both the flower and the leaves.

Chamomile: You can also use this plant's flowers to infuse a floral scent to your desserts like homemade ice-cream or jello.

Fruit salad - The fruit salad consists of many different varieties of fruits. It goes well with syrup or in its juices. This type of salad is an appetizer, an accompaniment salad, or a dessert salad. Fruit salads also go well with spices rather than herbs. For example, black pepper or paprika salt are excellent combinations for delightful fruit salads. They balance out the taste buds, so there is no sugar overload. Fruit like a mango does very well with a spicy chili flavor with just a hint of salt.

Ginger: Putting a little ginger in the syrup or the fruit juice will give it a fun kick to complement the sweetness.

Mint: Mint has a cooling effect that can take the edge off tart fruits like green apples.

Cayenne: This pepper brings the heat, but because it has minimal flavor, it allows the sweet essence of the fruit to shine through.

Cinnamon: Cinnamon is synonymous with sweet baked goodness. Candied fruits featuring cinnamon are not just delicious but also have an exciting kick.

You can make your homemade vinaigrette and refrigerate it for up to two weeks. And you can use a mix of herbs and spices to make it come alive.

HOW TO USE HERBS AND SPICES IN SNACKS

It is easy to include spice and herbs in your snack in two ways. You can prepare the bite with the spices and herbs in the recipe, common with baked goods. Alternatively, you can make a dip infused with fun spices and herbs to elevate the taste.

Preparing healthy snacks for yourself or your family needs a bit of creativity, so most people prefer to buy them. Unfortunately, store-bought snacks can have a lot of sodium or sugar in them. It is a better idea to create easy recipes for healthy snacks from the comfort of your home.

For example, consider cutting up fresh fruit and add some lime fruit to infuse some tartness. Then you can add some salted paprika. You can also cut up carrots and celery into sticks and make a Greek yogurt dip with mint. How about some avocado with a hint of cumin, cilantro, and lime? Herbs and spices add more texture to an ordinary fruit salad.

According to the CDC, American children between the ages of 6-18 consume 3,300 mg of sodium daily in the foodstuff they eat. And they may continue to add more salt at the table during mealtime. However, the recommended amount of salt for kids according to the Dietary Guidelines for Americans is 2,300 mg daily. Herbs and spices lessen the need to consume a lot of salt. Combining a healthy snack with a spice or herb-infused dip is one of the ways to do this.

Ginger: Add this spice to warmed fruit bits like peaches or sweet apples to give them a nice kick

Cilantro: Cilantro goes very well with creamy snacks like avocado, sour cream, or Greek yogurt. It breaks the creaminess by infusing a fresh flavor.

Pepper: Peppers infuse a spicy flavor to everything they touch, from fruit to popcorn and toasted almonds. The best part is that they blend well with most types of foods.

Cinnamon: This spice can be used topically on fruits and also on drinks like shakes. However, most people love it in baked goods. If you know how to bake using cinnamon in your recipes, this is a sure way to make snacks more interesting.

Nutmeg: Nutmeg, in a warm creamy drink, takes the flavor from standard to incredible. It is famous in eggnog, but it is also great in hot chocolate. Adults can also enjoy nutmeg laced wine for those with adventurous palates.

Cloves: Cloves have an overpowering flavor, but the spice works very well in baked goods. It injects a bit of spiciness into the sweetness of cakes and biscuits. And some people find that they use less sugar when they use cloves in their recipes.

HOW TO USE HERBS IN THE MAIN DISH

The main dish is the star of your dinner table. Salads and desserts vie for attention with your roast or pasta dish, so it has to be perfectly seasoned and flavored. The proper use of herbs and spices in the main dish typically means you use much less in the salads and desserts.

You will enjoy the art/science of cooking with spices and herbs the more you use them and learn the flavors. Some flavors are frequent in the main dish. Increasing your knowledge in using these spices will give you and your family a fresh take on ordinary meals every time you set the table.

Using spices and herbs doesn't mean that you have to change your daily menu. Keep cooking your usual dishes, but invite more aroma and flavor into the kitchen by consistently improving its taste with herbs and spices.

For example, most people love French fries, but they prepare the most basic dish versions. How about adding some dried basil and red pepper flakes into the recipe for a nice kick and flavor. And to even enhance it more, add a sliced half of red onion. Here are some of the common spices you need to transform any main dish:

Basil: The popular variety of basil used in cooking is sweet basil because it has a unique infuse of sweetness and pepperiness. You may even be able to taste a hint of mint in this herb. So if you were considering using mint leaves, you have to be very conservative with your measures.

Bay leaves: The mild flavor of this herb goes very well with soups and stews. It can be cooked for a long time to infuse even more flavor. However, you must remove these leaves when serving the dish. Bay leaves are very bitter.

Oregano: This herb is almost similar in aroma to bay leaves, so the two are interchangeable. However, oregano stays in the dish.

Peppers: From mild options like black pepper to heavy hitters like cayenne peppers, infuse a beautiful mix of heat and spiciness in any dish. Of course, you must use them in a very measured manner. Keep dried red chilies at hand to add flavor to your meals. When shopping for peppers, look for variety like smoked flavors, very hot flavors, and fruity aromas.

Coriander: You can use both the seeds and leaves of this plant. The seeds are excellent for rubbing into meats like lamb chops and ribs. Add the leaves to the dish at the very last minute of cooking to preserve their citrusy flavor. They can also be served raw and chopped up as a garnish to the dish.

Cinnamon: If you want to give a savory dish even more

flavor, drop a little cinnamon. It is a very aromatic and spicy flavored spice, and it tastes fantastic with root vegetables like carrots and parsnips.

Cumin: This is a herb with an outstanding balance of earthy and spicy flavors. It will transform bean dishes, curries and infuse excellent flavor in plain old rice.

Dill: This is one of those herbs that perform better when fresh compared to when dry. Fresh dill will brighten up any main dish, especially fish-based recipes. It also goes well with potatoes. You can also use it to pickle vegetables.

HOW TO USE SPICES AND HERBS IN DESSERTS

Spices and herbs in desserts bring summer into your mouth, even in the dead of winter. You can mix spices with maple syrup or honey and drizzle on top of any dessert. Or maybe place some pureed mint into a frosty glass of iced lemon tea for a sweet treat on a hot summer afternoon.

Rosemary: It may not be your first choice of herb in a dessert, but rosemary in a drink is delicious. It can be a hot drink or a cold one. It brings a sweet freshness to the beverage.

Mint: Mint in your mug of hot chocolate is a match made in heaven. If you are baking a chocolate cake, add in some mint. It also blends well with a scoop of vanilla or chocolate ice cream. Mint cuts through the rich flavors of vanilla and chocolate to give you a fresh taste.

Thyme: Thyme is an excellent choice when you are preparing heated desserts like grilled peaches. It brings a fresh citrusy flavor with a hint of mint to the hot dessert giving it perfect balance.

Vanilla: This is a staple in many kitchens because it transforms anything from basic tasting to creamy, warm deliciousness. You can use it in baking, preparing drinks, and dessert dips.

Nutmeg: Like vanilla, this spice is earthy with its distinct nutty flavor with a sweet, warm spiciness. It makes everything comfort food, and it works well when you want a dessert in a cozy environment.

"Spice is life. It depends upon what you like...have fun with it. Yes, food is serious, but you should have fun with it."

— *EMERIL LAGASSE*

BONUS CHAPTER: SALT - OFF-TOPIC, BUT ON TABLES

*I*f only humans were like salt, the world would most likely be a better place. Yes, we would be available for each other, living an affordable life, playing a vital role, and yes, bringing out the best in others, all in a pinch. Yet, we are not salt; we are only human.

Salt is not a spice or herb, but it is a condiment that can complement these ingredients, helping them to bring out their flavor. Savory foods need salt to enhance the taste, and some sugary drinks and foods use a pinch of salt to make them tastier.

Did you know that salt also preserves food? That is why most processed foods contain very high quantities of salt.

IS SALT THE MOST POPULAR CONDIMENT?

The word salad originated from the word salt as the ancient Romans used it to salt their vegetables and leafy greens. It was also the currency in different civilizations, and because of its monetary value, the phrase "Not worth his/her/its salt" came up. People quickly learned that food flavored with salt was tastier with or without the herbs and spices to accompany it. As a result, salt became the most popular condiment preferred even above spices and herbs.

If you are looking for proof of salt's popularity, all you have to do is look at the salt routes crisscrossing the globe. The routes included one from Morocco across the Sahara to Timbuktu, from Egypt to Greece, and Venice to Asia.

Interestingly, salt was also popular because it solidified one's status in society. At banquets, the place that one sat with regard to the saltcellar (salt container) showed their level of importance. If you sat at the table's head or before the salt cellar, you were distinguished and important. Anyone below or after the salt-cellar was inconsequential.

The popularity of salt is unrivaled because of its ability to season food. In ancient times, its ability to even prompt revolutions like the French revolt against King Louis XVI. Its rich history informs salt popularity for past centuries as well as in the present. Accounts have it that whole economies revolved around salt. For instance, can you imagine an entire regional route dedicated to salt transportation? Well, such was the case in the middle ages and the value that was attached to salt. One of the most famous of these roads exists until today and was known as the 'Old Salt Route' in Northern Germany. This route ran from the salt mines to shipping ports.

This commodity has a dedicated route to show how valuable and precious salt was to ancient civilization. In today's Wall Street, gold has always been the safest commodity to invest. Through cultures of the past, you could never have gone wrong investing in salt.

Salt production contributed significantly to the building of America. The first patent to produce salt in the colonies was Massachusetts Bay Colony held. It held that patent, but it also went on to make salt for the next 200 years.

For a commodity to be at the center of an uprising, it must be precious. Today we can equate a product of such significance to oil and precious metals necessary for the production of technology such as phones and laptops. One of the reasons for the French Revolution was anger over the salt tax introduced at the time. It was known as the gabelle, resulting in massive disparities in salt's cost throughout the different French regions. Since salt was used in cooking, making cheese, food preservation, and raising livestock, it affected every sphere of life and everyone in the country.

In March 1930, Gandhi and his followers marched for 23 days to protest their colonial master's monopoly. The British government was the only one allowed to produce and profit from the salt production conducted by Indians living on the coast. This march was christened 'the Salt March to Dand.'

Most impressive about salt historically is that it transcended daily use and economics to cultural and religious significance. Buddhists have long used it to repel evil. In Shintoism, salt purifies things, while In Judeo-Christian traditions, salt was used as an offering and to seal covenants and purify people and objects. Salt, alongside other precious commodities of the past such as myrrh, frankincense, and gold, managed to find its way into ancient religious texts such as the Bible. In

Genesis, the first book of the Old Testament, Lot's wife became a salt pillar after disobeying God's command. The rock-salt post still stands today on Mount Sodom and is christened 'Lot's Wife.'

In the New Testament, Jesus teaches that his believers are the salt of the earth, but if salt has lost its taste, how shall its saltiness be restored? It is no longer good for anything except to be thrown out and trampled under people's feet.' it makes me wonder why he did not say that you are the turmeric, cinnamon, or ginger of the earth. That is no knock on these beautiful and incredibly beneficial commodities. Still, it does go to show the incredible place and importance of salt culturally as well as spiritually across civilizations. Salt remains an essential and valuable commodity to this day.

IS SALT THE MOST ABUNDANT MINERAL?

Salt is one of the most abundant minerals on earth. It is derived from dried up, dead beds known as rock salt or from seawater. It bubbles up in brine in seawater, while rock salt is in shallow caverns and salt licks.

Salt is just below the earth's surface in white veins that can go down thousands of feet. The seams are evaporated from salt pans or mined from the shafts. Most of the time, animals wore paths to the nearest salt licks. So the people around began to follow the tracks made by animals as they went to the salt licks and made settlements around them.

Large salt rock deposits can be found worldwide from the United States and Canada to China, Germany, and India. China produces the most amount of salt worldwide.

TYPES OF SALT

NaCl - It is the common salt, also known as sodium chloride. It is known as table salt and comes from salt deposits. Treatment of

Sodium chloride entails using an anti-caking agent that prevents the salt from clumping.

Kosher salt – Kosher salt is grainier with coarse grains and has a flakier texture. Because the grains are larger, most people use it to salt meats, allowing the grains to release a fantastic blast of flavor. Kosher salt dissolves faster, so it is usable for all types of cooking.

Sea salt – Sea salt is directly evaporated from seawater and is typically unrefined. It contains more zinc, iron, and potassium, which gives the salt a complex flavor. People prefer to use it as table salt for a full flavor profile.

Fleur de Sel – This salt is known as flower salt, hand-harvested off the French coast in Brittany. It comes as paper-thin crystals that off the water surface like one would skim the cream off the top of milk. Because its harvest process is labor-intensive, this salt is the most expensive in the world. This salt retains moisture, and it comes with a grey-blue tint because of its high mineral content.

> **Himalayan pink salt** - It is the purest form of salt globally, and it is hand-harvested from the Khewra salt mine in Pakistan's Himalayan mountains. It is both a cooking and finishing salt because it has a bolder flavor. It has 84 minerals naturally occurring in it, giving it an exotic taste.

> **Kala namak** – It is Himalayan salt that has been packed in a jar together with charcoal, barks, seeds, and herbs. It is then fired in the furnace for 24 hours straight before it is cooled and stored. Finally, it is left to age for a while before using it. Kala namak has a red-black color, a sulfurous aroma, and a spicy, salty taste.

> **Black Hawaiian salt** – It is also known as lava salt, and it is a type of sea salt that comes from the volcanic island of Hawaii. Some activated charcoal is added to it to give it its flavor.

Red Hawaiian salt - There is also red Hawaiian salt that is unrefined and harvested from the island's volcanic red soil rich in iron. It is excellent for meat dishes or seafood.

Celtic Sea salt - This salt is known as grey salt, and it comes from the bottom of the tidal ponds found off the French coast. The crystals come out of the pond's bottom, and they have a briny taste. These crystals are moist and chunky with a grey hue.

Flaky salt – True to its name, this salt is flaky, so it is a finishing salt. It is white and delicate and offers a pop of flavor.

Pickling salt – The salt is useful for pickling as well as bringing. The pickling salt doesn't contain anti-caking agents, minerals, or iodine.

Smoked salt – This salt is slow-smoked for around two weeks over a wooded fire to add a smoky salt. The wood used will determine the salt's flavor and taste, and it is excellent for hearty foods like potatoes and meats.

Rock salt, Kosher salt, and Sea salt are composed of chlorine and sodium. They all comprise approximately 40 percent sodium by weight. They may contain additional potassium and other minerals but in small amounts. It is worth noting that salt and sodium occur naturally dissolved in seawater or as a crystalline solid in rock salt.

Most people may fail to realize that they take in too much salt and sodium without knowing, thanks to a high intake of processed, restaurant, and convenience store foods. Over and above the earlier mentioned areas where salt comes from, foods such as the following can have salt loads. The top six salty foods in the United States (U.S.), according to the American Heart

Association (AHA), are bread and rolls, Pizza, Cured meats and cold cuts, Sandwiches, Soup, and Poultry. While the body needs salt for proper function, too much or too little can cause problems.

SOURCES OF SODIUM CHLORIDE

We should all be grateful that various salt sources contribute to its abundance; otherwise, we would all still be fighting for it. However, as progressive as humans are, we would most likely be using synthetic salt. After all, we can produce just about anything. Thankfully, nature ensured we had an adequate supply. Sources of salt include:

Mined salt: It is salt mined from the mine. Deep shaft mining is like extracting any other minerals, and these miners use the room and pillar method of mining. That means that shafts sink into the mine floor with rooms constructed carefully by drilling, blasting, and cutting. The salt is removed and crushed, then sent to the surface via a conveyor belt.

Sea salt: Sea salt comes from evaporated seawater. It is one of the first salts used in prehistoric times, and since it is minimally refined, it contains higher levels of nutrients but not too much.

Dry lake salt: The dry lake salt comes from a flatbed of clay where the salt encrusts the earth. The salt lies on the surface, making it easier to extract. The dry lake can be small at less than one mile, while others are thousands of miles. They remain dry for a large part of the year.

HOW TO USE SALT AS A PRESERVATIVE

A long time ago, our ancestors used salt to preserve their food. Things have changed much since then, yet some remain the same. People worldwide still use salt as a preservative since it is one of the most tried and tested ways. Salt acts either as a drying agent or a microbe killing agent.

Salt dehydrates food by drawing the water out. As a result, the bacteria that cause food poisoning don't have a conducive environment to thrive in foods preserved with salt. The salt leaves the food completely dry.

Salt is also toxic to bacteria and microbes because it causes osmosis to occur in their cells. Because of the difference in the water pressure inside and outside their cells, the microbes will rupture. The salt also interferes with the internal processes of the bacterium. Sugar has the same effect as salt as a preservative.

SALT FOR HEALTH

Salt helps you stay hydrated by maintaining a balance between the outside and inside of the cells. That is important for the healthy functioning of body cells as it regulates the water inside and around the cells. It also promotes excellent vascular health and protects the heart's blood vessels by maintaining body-fluid volume and improving our blood's osmotic balance.

Salt prevents muscle cramping, especially after intense physical activity, by triggering nerve impulses to control the muscles' contractions. Low levels of sodium cause the nerves to get out of control, causing painful cramping.

Salt also promotes nervous system health because sodium electrolytes facilitate the transmission of nerve impulses within the body.

On the flip side, too much salt affects the kidneys' function because it frequently triggers the system to over-respond to electric stimuli. It also causes the heart to pump faster, causing hypertension and heart problems as the body works hard to remove excess fluid from the cells.

Have you ever noticed how sluggish you get after eating processed foods? That is because sodium depletes potassium levels, and when you are potassium deficient, you generally have low energy levels leaving you exhausted and chronically fatigued. As a result, you become easily irritable.

WHICH CONDITIONS CAN OVERUSE OF SALT LEAD TO?

High blood pressure

Too much salt raises the sodium in the bloodstream, which causes an imbalance in the cells. The result is elevated blood pressure as the blood vessels strain to remove the body's excess fluid. The effect on blood pressure depends on the individual. Some people will experience an instant elevation with even the smallest salt quantity, while others will show no signs for years.

Kidney disease

When there is a lot of salt in the system, the kidneys cannot function at optimum because there is a strain on their blood vessels due to high blood pressure. The continued stress may cause kidney disease in the long term.

Unfortunately, kidney disease means that your body is not able to filter your blood as it should. One is at a higher risk of kidney disease if you have hypertension, and salt is a leading contributor to high blood pressure. Also, people with heart disease may quickly find themselves battling kidney disease years down the line.

Obesity

High salt intake is associated with increased chances of

obesity. The elevated levels of salt cause you to want sweetened drinks, leading to a weight increase. Experts recommend lowering your intake of sodium-rich foods to have a healthy weight.

However, it is essential to make sure that you maintain a healthy balance of sodium to prevent other issues like electrolyte imbalance in the body. When the sodium and potassium levels in the body are too low, your body cells cannot function at their peak.

Heart disease

Blood pressure can impact your heart's healthy function as it causes it to work too hard. As a result, your heart becomes weaker and stops functioning at optimum. Most people with high blood pressure may not realize the impact the force of blood coursing through their veins is having on the ir heart function.

Elevated blood pressure levels that are left untreated and become a chronic condition will weaken the heart and damage your heart arteries. The inferior function of the heart is likely to lead to heart failure.

Osteoporosis

Salt causes a problem in calcium absorption. Calcium is crucial in healthy bones, so the more sodium you take, the higher the chances of osteoporosis. The more salt you consume, the more likely you are to lose calcium through your urine.

As you lose more calcium due to a sodium-rich diet, you end up losing bone strength. As the bones weaken, you will find yourself more susceptible to osteoporosis.

SALT AS A HEALER

Have you ever heard that the cure for anything is saltwater: the seas, tears, or sweat. Is there truth to that claim? If you understand the healing properties that salt is known for, you realize why salt is so respected as a healing compound.

The body requires minerals to work side by side with vitamins for cells to function correctly. Salt contains 92 trace minerals and 24 essential minerals, which help prevent deficiencies in our body. That could be anything ranging from the loss of control of ions, resulting in cell damage to muscle spasms, nervous disorder, and brain damage. Salt is the main reason our cells can function at optimum.

Take psoriasis and eczema, which are conditions that can be quite persistent and often refuse to respond to conventional medicine. Psoriasis is a skin condition in which the cells build up and form scabs and dry patches that are itchy. It is an immune system problem triggered by several things such as cold, stress, or infections. Eczema, on the other hand, is also a condition where patches of skin become inflamed, red, itchy, rough, and in some instances, cracked. At times blisters can occur.

Treatment of these diseases focuses on healing damaged skin and alleviating symptoms. As of yet, there is no full cure for the conditions, but signs are manageable. Part of that management involves salt. That explains why mineral-rich saltwater in places like the Dead Sea in the Middle East and the Blue Lagoon in Iceland helps with skin conditions.

Soaking in saltwater, such as in the locations mentioned above, helps moisturize the skin and ease redness. In psoriasis or eczema, these salt waters can help relieve the scaly patches and inflammation. You do not have to go all the way to the middle east to experience such relief; one can do this at home by adding Dead Sea salts, also known as Epsom salts, to your tub and soak for about 15 minutes. Surprisingly, even a cup of plain table salt in your bath water can ease eczema and psoriasis symptoms.

Other less severe conditions can also experience soothing as a result of using salt. Swishing water and salt can heal oral situations such as mouth cankers. A saltwater rinse can improve your oral health by reducing bacteria that can cause mouth sores and sore throats. Salt is also useful in fighting bad breath.

Since salt is a readily available ingredient, it is also regularly used to maintain oral health. It removes particles of food from the mouth as it flushes the mouth cavity.

Salt can also bring relief to a constipated person when you are unable to have a bowel movement. Dissolving some Epsom salt in a glass of water, usually 2-6 teaspoons, can help you go as soon as half an hour to six hours. If the solution is unpalatable, adding some lemon juice can help with the taste.

Epsom salt helps relieve migraines as well as joint pain. That is possible because this salt contains two vital elements, namely, magnesium and sulfate. These elements facilitate the muscles' proper functioning and the nerves in your body, making salt baths excellent for the skin and reducing joint pain and arthritis. The magnesium in the salt has anti-inflammatory properties, while the sulfate encourages the absorption of nutrients into the skin.

In the medicine cabinet or the spice rack, salt can always have a place in our homes. And it usually does. The balance between using the right amount of salt and going overboard in its use is delicate. Herbs and spices complement the salt's use marvelously because you will find that the more herbs you use, the less salt you need in your food. That is why experts in the kitchen always work with a pinch of salt.

> *"The cure for anything is saltwater - sweat, tears or the sea ."*
>
> — *KAREN BLIXEN*

FINAL WORDS

The role of spices and herbs is undeniable. My appreciation of delicious food has been enhanced over the years as I continually delve into herbs and spices in my cooking and food prep.

This book has illustrated that fresh herbs are excellent for garnishing your dishes, and dried herbs give more potency.

It has shown that our expectations only limit spices and herbs. They are nature's ever-present cures to some of the ailments we suffer daily. In some cases, they have inspired science to find synthetic solutions to sickness.

They hold the promise of a world where we can protect our well being while enjoying a healthy dish.

Together, we have highlighted the importance of herbs and spices in living your best life. We have brought to the fore the importance of using these natural plants to find health and, by extension, wealth.

The overall goal is knowing that this resource has helped you gain more insight into herbs and spices' benefits. Hopefully, it inspires you to use it to further your personal experience with these plants.

That is the whole point of sharing this knowledge; it is a

stepping stone to the best version of you and absolute enjoyment of food.

The Spice of Life illustrates how delicious and aroma-filled you will find life to be dining on the rainbow. Herbs and spices add zest to our food, improving palatability while enhancing flavor and health benefits. We can improve the quality and quantity of our lives by merely embracing healthy options. The good news is that we have herbs and spices to accompany us throughout our journey. As long as we purpose to walk the path, a better world will emerge for ourselves and our loved ones.

We can change the way this and future generations will perceive food and life. The time to spice up our lives, have exciting foods and drinks, enjoy natural healing, and add some flavor to our lives is now. Do not be left behind!

> *"Healing has to be consistent with life itself. If it isn't, then it's not healing. The healing components have to be from life. "*
>
> *— DR. SEBI*

GLOSSARY

AILMENTS OVERVIEW

Stroke: A stroke is a result of interruption of blood flow to part of your brain. This causes the brain cells deprived of oxygen to begin to die off within a matter of minutes.

Diabetes: A condition caused by elevated levels of sugar in your blood.

Atherosclerotic heart disease: This condition affects the arteries in the heart because of buildup of plaque inside the artery wall. The plaque is brought on by high cholesterol levels.

Cognitive disorders: These are conditions that affect one's cognitive abilities. They are commonly referred to as NCDs and they include symptoms like dementia, amnesia and cognitive impairment.

Alzheimer's disease: A condition affecting the brain cell connections causing the brain cells to degenerate and die. As a result, one suffers memory loss and decline in functionality.

Obesity: Obesity is more complex than just an excessive amount of fat in the body. It increases the risk of heart disease, cancer, diabetes and high blood pressure.

Irritable Bowel Syndrome: This condition affects the large intestines and it is a chronic condition. It comes with bloating, diarrhea, abdominal pain, gas, constipation and cramping.

Indigestion: Indigestion is characterized by among many other symptoms acid reflux (heartburn), stomach discomfort, decrease in appetite, nausea and constipation.

Anxiety: An anxiety disorder is a mental health condition in which one experiences overwhelming feelings of worry, fear and uncertainty. These feelings are so intense crippling you and making it hard for you to function normally.

SPICES AND HERBS OVERVIEW

Ajwain (Umbelliferae): Ajwain encompasses over 2,700 spices including cumin, dill and caraway. It is also known as carom or bishop's weed.

Aleppo pepper (Capsicum annul): Native to northwestern Syria, this pepper has a delicate Mediterranean flavor. It is also known as Halaby pepper.

Allspice (Pimienta): It has several aromas rolled into it. It mimics ginger, nutmeg, cloves, and cinnamon and it exclusively grows in the rainforests of South and Central America and the Caribbean.

Anise (Pimpinella anisum): The distinct licorice flavor of this herb is extracted from its essential oil. It is one of the oldest spices used across continents. The seeds are the ones harvested and they look brownish red or grayish green and have a ribbed texture.

Ashwagandha (Withania somnifera): Also known as Indian ginseng, winter cherry or poison gooseberry this is an evergreen shrub growing in the Middle East, Africa and of course India. The root is the one used and it has a strong pungent scent. Some say it smells like a horse.

Achiote: It has a hint of nutmeg and is peppery in flavor. This spice also infuses the food with a beautiful rich reddish yellow color. It is also used to color foodstuff like cheeses and butter.

Basil (Ocimum basilicum: This is an annual herb with a sweet yet peppery flavor. It thrives in the summer months and infuses the food with warmth and a refreshing flavor.

Bay leaf (Laurus Nobilis): This herb is indigenous to Asia but it has found its way to other parts of the world. It has a strong aroma and it also has a bitter taste.

Berbere (Aframomum corrorima): It infuses a spicy flavor when rubbed into meats, both white and red. You can also use it as a base for flavoring your curries, stews and soups.

Cumin (Cuminum cyminum): This herb has a fragrance similar to caraway. But this is because caraway is also from the same plant family and it is even known as Persian cumin. Cumin is popular in very highly flavored foods. It has a bit of a bite so you can find it in rice dishes as well as meat dishes.

Cilantro (Coriandrum Savitum): cilantro and coriander are one and the same spice. This herb has a sweet, citrusy flavor and is very refreshing in any dish.

Cinnamon (Cinnamomum verum): Cinnamon is derived from the bark of the cinnamon tree. The tree is an evergreen shrub also known as the Ceylon tree. The spice is sweet and spicy and has a strong aroma.

Cloves (Syzygium aromaticum): cloves are dried aromatic flower buds which end up resembling nails. This spice has an overpowering scent that is very spicy. It is popular in Mediterranean and Indian dishes and beverages.

Dill (Anethum graveolens): Dill belongs to the celery family and both its leaves and seeds are used in cooking. This means it can be used as both a spice and a herb.

Fennel (Foeniculum vulgare): Fennel is a member of the carrot family which means it is hardy with a bulb. All parts of this plant are edible from the bulb, stalks and leaves. It becomes soft and sweet when cooked.

Ginger (Zingiber officinale): It has a sweet warm yet pungent aroma and it can get very spicy when used in large quantities. Used in main dishes it brings out the flavor of meats but it can also be used in soups and stew not forgetting beverages.

Grains of Paradise (Aframomum melegueta): It is also known as Guinea pepper and it has a spicy flavor with a strong aroma. It has hints of ginger and cardamom and also infuses a pepperiness to dishes.

Juniper (Juniperus): Juniper berries are black in color. They have a piney scent and the rest of the plat can be used to freshen stale air. You may experience the scent of gin or turpentine when you cook with the seeds. They are also bittersweet.

Lemon verdana (Aloysia citrodora): This herb is from the verbena family and it injects a refreshing taste to beverages especially cold ones. The penetrating lemony flavor of the herb makes it popular with seafood dishes because it doesn't lose its flavor even with cooking.

Lemongrass (Cymbopogon): The long stalks of this plant have the same essential oil found in lemon peels. This is what gives it the lemon flavor and you can use the lower end of the stalk for cooking. It gives the dish a vibrant scent.

Nutmeg and Mace (Myristica fragrans): this is a tropical plant evergreen in nature. Nutmeg is the seed while mace is the covering of the seed. Mace is much more valuable compared to nutmeg but they both have the sweet nutty fragrance. However, mace is more aromatic than nutmeg.

Mint (Mentha): The menthol flavor of this herb makes

it a favorite when for refreshing dishes. This herb is used to refresh the sense whether in food or with topical use.

Myrtle (Myrtus): This herb has a hint of rosemary and juniper and the leaves are bitter and astringent in nature. The almost citrusy aroma which is refreshing and clean.

Tarragon (Artemisia dracunculus): The herb is a perennial plant and it is cultivated for its aromatic scent. It smells fresh and has a similar herbal composition to fennel and basil.

Turmeric Curcuma Longa: This is an ancient spice with an acrid scent. It is part of the ginger herb family so it can be used for both culinary and medicinal purposes.

Thyme: This is a staple herb in most traditional dishes. It has a delicate savoriness and it can also be used in all types of casseroles, stews and soups. The delicate scent has a faraway sweetness.

SOURCES

https://extension.psu.edu/herb-and-spice-history
https://www.mccormickscienceinstitute.com/resources/history-of-spices
https://www.nationalgeographic.com/news/2017/05/history-origin-of-saffron-spice-iran/
https://www.cs.mcgill.ca/~rwest/wikispeedia/wpcd/wp/h/History_of_saffron.htm
http://www.todayifoundout.com/index.php/2014/01/brief-history-pepper/
https://www.ozy.com/around-the-world/the-hidden-history-of-scandinavias-love-of-cardamom/82046/
https://www.myspicer.com/history-cardamom/
https://www.thespruceeats.com/history-of-cinnamon-1807584
https://www.vedanet.com/herbs-for-the-practice-of-yoga-1-introduction/
https://www.hindawi.com/journals/ecam/2013/617459/
https://www.verywellhealth.com/traditional-chinese-medicine-what-you-need-to-know-88936
https://www.healthline.com/health/gotu-kola-benefits
https://www.webmd.com/heart-disease/news/20040503/do-antioxidants-contribute-to-heart-disease
https://www.ncbi.nlm.nih.gov/pmc/articles/PMC5318325/

https://www.healthline.com/nutrition/coriander-benefits#8.-Easy-to-add-to-your-diet
https://www.healthline.com/health/health-benefits-of-thyme
http://pennstatehershey.adam.com/content.aspx?productid=107&pid=33&gid=000271
https://www.ncbi.nlm.nih.gov/pubmed/17487414
https://www.ncbi.nlm.nih.gov/pubmed/17827696
https://www.ncbi.nlm.nih.gov/pubmed/16213119
https://www.ncbi.nlm.nih.gov/pmc/articles/PMC6368199/
https://www.healthline.com/nutrition/9-benefits-of-cumin#section5
https://www.ncbi.nlm.nih.gov/pubmed/25456022
https://www.academia.edu/8628985/Saffron_in_the_treatment_of_patients_with_mild_to_moderate_Alzheimer_s_disease_a_16-week_randomized_and_placebo-controlled_trial_Saffron_in_the_treatment_of_Alzheimer_s_disease
https://www.ncbi.nlm.nih.gov/pubmed/29589534
https://www.organicconsumers.org/sites/default/files/what%27s%20wrong%20with%20food%20irradiation.pdf
http://https//www.ncbi.nlm.nih.gov/pubmed/24015007
http://https/www.ncbi.nlm.nih.gov/pmc/articles/PMC3310143/
http://https/www.ncbi.nlm.nih.gov/pmc/articles/PMC4299449/
https://www.cdc.gov/vitalsigns/children-sodium/index.html
http://theepicentre.com/spices/
https://www.youtube.com/watch?v=d5OtqoZ4Wz8